# Invisible on Thursdays

# Invisible on Thursdays

## an esoteric journey

## Peppy Barlow

**Bridge House**

British Library Cataloguing in Publication Data
A Record of this Publication is available from the British
Library

ISBN 978-1-914199-16-5


This edition published 2022 by Bridge House Publishing
Manchester, England

Cover illustration: *The Fool* © Nicki Holt

Illustration for "Visible": *Orpheus* © Nicki Holt

# Contents

# INTRODUCTION

While I was writing this someone asked me what kind of book it was? I found myself saying, 'It's not a book, it's a vase.' To me it had become a solid object, a series of patterns and pictures etched in clay.

The main body of the text is a journey I made with a dear friend – first called Persephone (Persey), later Lucia. We met on a windy hill in Kent where my sister had killed herself and began exploring the meaning of our lives together. We talked about family, work and children and employed all kinds of esoteric tools looking for patterns in our lives. She was interested in astrology. I had inherited my sister's Tarot cards and a book about hand reading. Later we travelled to Greece (to Crete) where our names originated and spent a year contemplating myths, landscape and the need for love in our lives. Persey found a suitable mate and went back to England. I stayed on until the end of the year and came home to live in Suffolk where I ran a tearoom and began my writing. Later, I explored past life healing. Lucia joined me on this journey for a while before she went back to Greece to run a hotel with her sons. For many years we only saw each other intermittently. But then there was a phone call from Greece and she was on her way back home to fight ovarian cancer.

We didn't let that faze us at all to begin with – after all, didn't we have every form of power and wisdom at our disposal? We tried everything: myth, magic, religion, strange potions, every kind of healing, as well as conventional chemotherapy, which we imbued with meaning. For a couple of years it worked but then the cancer came back and Lucia decided not to go through with any more chemo. So then we attended to her passage into death. It was an extraordinary journey full of tears and rage and laughter.

So why the vase? Well, apart from the main story, which in itself is often more about moments than narrative, there are three other layers. At the top of each chapter there are the names of the Major Arcana from the Tarot – a journey in itself. Below those are pieces of writing that relate to my experiences at the time. Along the end of each chapter are sections of the last letter my sister wrote to my mother during her travels round the Middle East, before she came home to die. Patterns running round the top and bottom of the vase; separate journeys which are somehow deeply connected and lend colour and meaning to each other.

The final chapter is an account of my return to Crete, to the place Lucia and I had lived in all those years ago. This, to me, seemed to create a lid. So, perhaps not so much a vase, as a Grecian Urn.

**Peppy Barlow**

*THE STAGE IS DARK*
*THE VOICES OF CHILDREN*
*DIANA IS SIX. CASSANDRA IS FOUR. JASON IS THREE.*

**DIANA:** *Visible. I can see them. The birds. The flying. Butterflies. I can see birds and leaves falling. I can see.*

**CASSANDRA:** *Invisible. They can't see me. I call to them. They can't hear me. I am here. They look at me. They look through me.*

**JASON:** *They see me.*

**DIANA:** *This is my garden. I don't want them here. I must run.*

**JASON:** *I can see her running.*

**DIANA:** *I must run and hide.*

**CASSANDRA:** *She has gone. Up into the trees with the birds. I know she can see me.*

**JASON:** *Socks. They let me out in my socks. I can't run in my socks.*

**DIANA:** *My garden. Mine. I am first.*

**CASSANDRA:** *They wanted a boy. I am not the boy.*

**JASON:** *I can't climb in my socks.*

**DIANA:** *Visible.*

**CASSANDRA:** *Invisible.*

**DIANA:** *Butterflies.*

**CASSANDRA:** *Birds.*

**JASON:** *Boy.*

**DIANA:** *I am here. High in the branches. They can't see me here. They can't reach me now. I am safe.*

BROKEN

# THE MAGICIAN

*This morning*
*I got out of bed at five o'clock*
*Came into the room with the Rayburn*
*Got out a pen and a notepad*
*And sat at the table by the window*
*Waiting for the dawn*

*It was there*
*And I had not seen it come*
*The light*
*Drawing the fields out of darkness*
*Sheep quietly grazing*
*Across the surface of the land*

*I sit and wait*
*Wondering why I am still alive*
*If I am alive*
*Or merely a shape*
*Deposited each morning by the light*
*A figure in another landscape*

*ELMSTEAD 1978*

I am outside the gates of the village school. Waiting for my son to emerge so I can drive home and get on with – who knows what I was getting on with in those days. A bit of writing. A lot of trying to reorder my life in my head. A ritual walk round the hill while he was at school. I really had nothing I had to be doing but somehow every moment mattered. I had convinced myself that drawing in and concentrating, even when I didn't know what on, would make things happen. I was like a child who thinks if you wish hard enough the world will bend to your will.

I see him. He is wandering in the playground, chatting to a friend, completely oblivious of the boiling cauldron that is his mother standing fifty feet away.

'Adam,' I call to him, 'come on now. I've got things to do.'

He doesn't seem to hear, or he has learnt to edit me out. I shout louder.

'Adam, get over here, now.'

One or two of the mothers turn and look at me. I can see remarks being passed.

Adam looks in my direction but he doesn't move. He just stands there looking as though I am a feature in the landscape or a summer squall. Something he can do nothing about. Something he's got used to.

This time I shriek, 'Adam get in this bloody car right now or I'll go home without you!'

He looks at his friend as if to say, 'Oh well, I better go or my mum will explode,' and begins moving towards me.

Mothers watch him as he passes. He walks towards me cloaked in their silent sympathy.

'Now that's a woman I could be friends with,' a voice at my side.

I turn to see a small, dark woman dressed in Wellington boots, jeans and a battered Barbour jacket held together with string. She is much shorter than me but there is a sort of concentrated energy that emanates from her. Two black button eyes that have me fixed to the spot.

'Everyone else thinks I'm invisible. You seem to exist,' she says.

'That's a very odd thing to say. Of course I exist.'

To be honest I am a little scared to find someone else in my landscape, someone alive at least.

'Then what's all the shouting about? If you exist you can whisper,' she says.

'He doesn't seem to hear me if I don't yell at him.'

'He hears you. We can all hear you. You make enough noise to waken the dead.'

'Shit, am I making a spectacle of myself?' I say.

'I wouldn't worry. I don't exist either,' she says, 'You want to come back for a cup of tea?'

I could have said, 'Oh no, I have to go home and concentrate on bending reality to my will.' Instead I say, 'Yes.'

My new friend gets into a battered Land Rover with a girl and two boys and I follow her back through the lanes. It is spring. White blossom in the hedgerows. Daffodils planted under the trees by the side of the road. There were daffodils when my sister died. When we drove to the funeral. It must have been this time of year. I thought then, I still think, how can anyone want to die when there are daffodils?

The Land Rover stops outside a beamed cottage with a broken gate and she unpacks children and a sack of animal feed. A ragged dog stands at the gate wagging its tail. A couple of chickens are patrolling something which looks like a Belfast sink with bits of cast iron farm machinery attached to it.

To begin with Adam won't get out of the car. Thinking about it now he probably found any alteration in my mad routine quite unsettling. I don't yell at him this time. Just tell him he can come in and play and we will go home soon.

The others are waiting for us by the gate and we all process up to the front door with the dog and chickens taking up the rear.

Indoors, the kind of chaos that children and animals and art demand. Her husband is an artist she tells me. A sculptor. Author of the sink in the front garden and other works about the house. She had been a fabric designer

11

before they started having children. There are two goats and a pony out the back, she adds, as a sort of afterthought.

She moves a dog bowl off the table and pushes odd bits of bridle to one side before putting the kettle on. Adam has disappeared to explore with the boys and we are alone.

We talk. She says she had noticed me at the school for several weeks. She thought I looked rather standoffish and wasn't sure whether to approach me. And then today, the shouting had been so loud she thought I might need protection and had come over.

Protection seemed an odd word for her to use and then I thought, perhaps that is what I needed. I felt very exposed up there on the hill alone in my little cottage. Perhaps I was shouting to fill the space. Hoping someone would hear me.

'You don't look as though you have much in common with the crowd outside the school gate,' she says.

'Nor do you,' I say.

'I'm forever having their children round for tea and play and rides on the pony but they never ask my kids back.'

'I don't ask them round.'

'Well, you may have it right.'

'Only because I think it might take up too much of my time.'

'Oh, sorry,' she says, fixing me with her black button eyes. 'Am I taking your precious time?'

'No, no, I didn't mean that. It's just that I am writing a book. I keep thinking if I can just get it finished I will be able to go back out into the world again.'

'What world is that then?'

'I used to be a journalist, before I had Adam. In Ireland. I lived with another journalist and his children... and... then I fell in love with someone else... chaos. This is like being on a retreat. I don't know how else to get things back in order.'

'Order, now that's something I don't worry much about,' she says, glancing round the kitchen.

I don't say anything. I don't tell her how I walk the hill each day and go into the church and don't exactly pray but walk round and round saying a mantra which is supposed to bring about the realisation of all you wish for.

'I see you walking round the hill, same every day,' she says. 'See you when I'm going to take the eggs to the shop. Is that part of your getting things back in order?'

I look at her. Is she watching me? Can she see me? This is odd.

'My name is Persephone, by the way,' she says. 'Persey for short. I'm thinking of changing it.'

'My name is Peppy, short of Penelope. It really annoys me, the name they gave me. Always waiting for someone to turn up.'

'How do you mean?'

'You must know the story. Her husband Odysseus goes away to fight in the Trojan Wars and doesn't come back for twenty years. While she waits she is solicited by suitors who want her and her kingdom. But she tells them she is weaving the winding sheet for her father-in-law and will only choose when she has finished the work. Every day she weaves and every night she unpicks it so that she doesn't have to make a choice. Endless bloody waiting.'

'Oh, who are you waiting for?'

'Anyone'll do,' I lie.

In truth I am still waiting for the fallout from Ireland. The man I had abandoned my life for in the hope that he would realise he couldn't live without me. He was showing no signs so far.

'We're all waiting for someone,' Persey says.

I look at her. She's looking down at the mug in her hands.

13

'But you're married.'

'That's what I thought.'

She doesn't seem to want to say anything more.

We go outside to find the children. Just by the back door there is a moulded bronze of her pregnant self. One of her husband's works of art.

'What do you think?' she asks as she turns to find me looking at it.

'Looks like a spare,' I say without thinking.

'That's rather how I feel,' she says, casually putting her hand on the swollen belly. 'I don't think I can have any more children.'

A little bit later, with dusk falling and the children parked in front of the television, she says, 'Have you had your chart read?'

'My what?'

'Your astrological chart.'

'I read the silly things in the paper sometimes but they're just for fun. I did take one quite seriously when I was about to leave Ireland. It said something about going on a journey to find out who I really was. I was on my way here.'

'I've been to an astrologer,' Persey says. 'I'm learning how to do it. Can I have a go at yours – before I get to know you too well?'

Another lunatic looking for signs from the gods. This was hopeful.

'I'm learning the Tarot,' I say, offering my madness in exchange. 'I've got my sister's pack and a couple of books. They scare me to death.'

'Scare you, why?'

'I don't know. I feel they have some kind of hidden power. I lay them out. I consult the book. And then Adam wants something and I don't like leaving them lying there

14

on the table when I'm not in the room. I feel as though they may come alive and go out into the world to create havoc. Alright, I know, I'm mad.'

'You think she saw it coming?' Persey asks after a short pause.

'What?'

'I've heard about it. We all have.'

'Oh that. I don't know. She talked about dying a lot. Had been talking about it for as long as I can remember. We stopped taking any notice.'

'But she did it.'

'Father always said she would cry wolf once too often.'

'Must have taken courage.'

'I suppose so.'

My sister, Charlotte, had died just before I arrived home. She was babysitting for my brother and his wife. They also had a house on the top of the hill. They went out. They came home. They had made up a bed for her in the study. The room with the guns. They heard something in the night. They thought it was the wind. It was a wild night. She had taken a gun. Walked out into the wind and the rain. Walked to the corner where the road fell down into the valley. Climbed a barbed wire fence and shot herself. The local farmer found her the next day. He spotted her sheepskin coat. Thought it was one of his animals in trouble.

I passed the place every day on my walk. Out across the top of the hill, down into the valley and up past the bend in the road with a view out to the horizon where a line of trees seemed to stand on the edge of the world. A thorn tree in the field where she was found. This is where she left from.

'If you're going to die, that is a beautiful spot,' I say.

We sit in silence.

'So give me your birth details and I'll see what I can do,' Persey says after a while.

15

I wondered then if it was a good idea. Did your fate run out in front of you like a giggling child until it delivered you to the edge of an abyss? Had my sister looked too far and not liked what she'd seen? Did I really want to know? 'Course,' I say.

---

**Last letter from Charlotte to her mother, January 1977**
*(During her travels Charlotte had converted to Islam.)*

*POSTE RESTANTE, MASHAD, IRAN*
*Dear Mum,*
*Now in Kerman which is very wild: the first real town except for Mahan where I spent last night, on the long desert run from Zaidan. Had to hitch-hike as had no money changed and the drivers were great – fed me up to the eyeballs as usual (they sort of gang together and about 6 trucks usually all stop at one place for chai and meals). However, at dinner they messed me about a bit so I insisted on going to a hotel that was in Mahan (40 kilometres from here). The only hotel in the town, which has an extremely beautiful mosque in which I spent a couple of hours today before coming here, was £10 plus a night so, of course, I was given my room with bathroom attached for free. It was heaven – virgin white sheets, central heating so I could dry all my clothes which I obviously washed (it's not so easy to do washing when it's cold, as now, for obvious reasons – i.e. it stays wet!!) and I hadn't had a REAL shower since leaving Mashad around a month ago so spent a good half hour under that.*

---

16

# THE HIGH PRIESTESS

*Where I walk*
*There is chalk*
*In the hedgerows*
*Today I wrote*
*ATARAXIA*
*On the harsh*
*Grained surface*
*Of the road*
*But only another*
*Foot traveller*
*Will see it*

*ELMSTEAD 1978*

Some time later I am sitting in Persey's kitchen again. The children are at school. In front of me there is what I know to be an astrological chart. A double circle with arcane signs and lines like a school geometry exercise. Persey is leaning over my shoulder. I can smell the familiar tang of horse and harness. I had found her out the back with the pony.

'It's very odd,' she says. 'Nearly everything is above the ascendant. You should be the most gregarious person in the world.'

'That doesn't make any sense,' I say. 'I live completely on my own, apart from Adam of course, and I only know a few people round here, apart from you...'

'Well perhaps you've come to explore the empty part of your chart, perhaps you're sailing through uncharted waters. There's lots of water here, hardly any earth. You could be lost at sea.'

That made a kind of sense. My dreams were full of raging seas that threatened to drown me. My whole life was

17

taken up with trying to find my way out of this strange place I find myself in. I am Penelope during the day, waiting for Odysseus to come home from the wars. Odysseus at night, beating my way back through the islands, trying to find my way home.

I had come back to Kent. Come home. My mother lived in a 14th century farm house at the bottom of the hill. My brother and his family are living within sight of my cottage. I'd bought the cottage because it was close and I thought coming home to my family would bring me back to myself. But it didn't feel as though I had arrived anywhere. 'Lost at sea' was a good way of describing it.

'So now it's your turn,' she says.

'What?'

'Did you bring the cards?

I had. They were burning a hole in my pocket but I was reluctant to take them out.

'I've only read a book. I don't think I know too much about them really,' I say.

'Who cares?' she says. 'Who said there was only one way of doing things? We can make it up as we go along.'

This was heresy to me. I liked to get things right. To know the rules. It was my sister who went round the world on her own. Became a Muslim. Prayed with the men in the mosques. Claimed she was never coming home. She would jump into a raging sea without a second thought. I was more likely to stand on the shore and watch. I got the cards out anyway. They had come to me wrapped in a white silk scarf which smelt strangely of the desert.

'What do you want to know?' I ask as I spread the scarf on the kitchen table.

'Anything. Everything. I want to know what my life is about?' says Persey.

'Not a lot then!' I say, as she pulls up a chair beside me.

18

I shuffle the cards. She shuffles the cards. She cuts the cards. I lay them out in the formation I've learnt from the book. We sit looking at the backs of them. Waiting to turn them over. I remember being very aware of the dust motes in a shaft of sunlight. A torn envelope on the table with a list scribbled on it. *Apples, Bread, Chicken feed.* The sound of the dog lapping water from a steel bowl that rattled on the stone floor.

'Which one do we turn over first?' she asks.

I reach for the first card I've laid. The one in the middle.

'This,' I say, 'is supposed to tell you what the question is about.'

'I haven't asked a question.'

'Then I think the card is supposed to tell you what's going on. You need my sister if you want a proper reading.'

'Oh for God's sake, Peppy, turn the bloody thing over and stop behaving as though they're going to bite you,' she says.

I turn over the card.

'Oh dear.'

Think she says that. I just look at the card. The image is of a knight lying on a stone slab with a sword beside him, three swords set on the wall above. *The Four of Swords.*

'Looks as though I'm dead already,' Persey says.

'No, I don't think it means that. It looks to me as though you are spending a night in the chapel before you go out to fight. A sort of vigil,' I offer. Really I have no idea.

'If you say so. Let's look at the next one.'

I turn over another card. *The Ace of Cups.*

'That's better. What's that one mean?'

'This is what's standing in your way,' I say.

'Oh, it looks good to me.'

'Could be that you are a warrior and waiting for love is holding you up?'

19

'You mean, I should pick up my sword and fight my way out?' she asks.

'Sounds a bit drastic,' I say. 'What's wrong with your marriage anyway?'

'Finish reading these first.' She is locked in concentration now and I have no idea whether I am reading things right.

'So the next card,' I say, consulting the layout I had copied it from the book, 'is supposed to tell you what your conscious self is aware of.'

The dog comes up and puts his head on her lap. I think he is feeling the tension.

I turn the card. A man in a cloak is standing on a desolate shore. There are three overturned cups in front of him and two upright cups on the ground behind him. *The Five of Cups*. Persey is looking at me. I feel as though I'm letting her down.

'Think fives are always difficult,' I say, 'but he isn't looking at the ones he's got, only at what he hasn't. He could turn round and there are two full cups behind him.'

'So, I'm looking in the wrong direction?'

'I dunno, I'm just saying what I see.'

'Next one,' she demands.

I reach for the card at the bottom. A man on a horse with a coin in his hand.

'Ah,' she says, picking it up. '*The Knight of Pentacles*. He looks like a likely contender. Nice horse. What do you think?' she asks the dog.

'That's what your unconscious is up to,' I say. 'Looking for a chap with his feet on the ground, a man with a bit of cash. More useful than love perhaps.'

'Money and a horse, I could cope with that!'

'Or a car,' I suggest.

'A fast car would be nice.' She relaxes a little, scratches the dog's head.

'Now, the next one is yourself in relation to the question,' I say, checking with the layout.

I turn over the *Ten of Pentacles*. An archway. Buildings. An old man and two white dogs in the foreground, a younger couple with a child under the arch. Pentacles all over the picture.

'Lots of money, I like that,' she says, picking up the card and looking closely at it.

'And dogs. I wouldn't want to be without a dog.'

'Suggests you have all the resources you need,' I say.

'If I had that kind of money I would be on the other side of the world,' she says, still holding the card.

'Really?'

'Wouldn't you?'

'I'm not sure I'm fit to travel.' I say, more or less to myself.

'If you could go anywhere, where would it be?' Persey asks.

'Where would you go?' I ask.

'This looks like Italy. I like Italy. David and I went there for a whole summer when we were students, painting frescoes. It was wonderful.'

'Greece,' I say. 'My mother sent me on an archaeological cruise with some friends when I was sixteen. I have memories of a moonlit supper in Crete and my first kiss. Greece would be my choice.'

'I always think of Greece as full of unattended ruins and old women on donkeys,' Persey remarks.

'Our names are Greek.'

She turns over the next card. A man leaving the battlefield with the spoils of war. *The Seven of Swords.*

'Now that looks a bit ominous,' I say. 'Someone is stealing away from the battlefield with what he can salvage.'

'Depends who gets the spoils,' Persey says with a slightly wicked look in her eye as she gets up to turn down a pot that is boiling on the stove.

Chicken food. I think. Another familiar smell.

She comes back. 'And this lot, the ones up the side, what are they going to tell me?'

'I think that's to do with what's going to happen next. Sort of prediction,' I say.

'Oh well, I suppose we better go on, although I'm not terribly impressed with the prognosis so far.'

I turn over the first card. *The Three of Cups*. Three women dancing.

'Well, that looks a bit better,' she says sitting down at the table again.

'Celebration, friends, often means relationship.'

The next card is *The King of Wands*. She laughs. 'And now a man with a big staff. Think I can add it to the man with the car and the money or is he the same person do you think?'

I turn the next card. *The Five of Swords*. Not so good.

'That's always a difficult one,' I say. 'My sister used to say it appears just as you've decided to do something, made a plan. Then someone, often a complete stranger, comes along and tells you you'll be making the biggest mistake of your life. She told me that the last time she read my cards. Before I left Ireland. That was the last time I saw her.'

'I don't think we're going to take your sister's word for much at this stage do you?' she says.

I look at her locked into the cards. Note that she's not that interested in my journey to this place. I think of my sister, her long dark hair obscuring her face as she lays the cards out on the kitchen table in the house in Dublin. The house I had shared with Adam's father.

'And I suppose she was right,' I say almost to myself.

22

'Last card, go on,' Persey insists.

I turn it over. *The King of Swords.*

'Another king. Surely that's auspicious,' she says.

'That's head stuff. *The King of Wands* is fire and passion. *The King of Pentacles* is earth, grounding. *The King of Swords* is telling you to use your head.'

'Oh well, not so bad I suppose. At least I'm not still lying about in a chapel like a dead person. What you think?'

'Sometimes they seem to make sense. Other times... I think I need to read some more books.'

'Perhaps we're both going on a journey,' she says for no particular reason. 'Perhaps we both need to find a way back home?'

---

*The desert was very beautiful – mountains to begin with, then dry flat plains with occasional weird bumps, made by the winds, which looked like moon craters. I have (so far) a great affinity with camels of which I am very proud as they normally let none but their owners approach them without spitting and being generally objectionable. There was an enormous one in Afghanistan which all the locals said was very fierce and dangerous, so of course I made immediate friends with it and rode it – it got up instantly, too, which was a great compliment.*

---

# THE EMPRESS

*I only know her*
*From photographs*
*But I can smell her still*
*Warm skin*
*And washed cotton*
*And sometimes*
*I think I can hear her*
*Singing to me*
*A lullaby in a language*
*I must once have known*

*ELMSTEAD 1978*

Trying to find our way back home was what we both seemed to be about. Wherever home was. Both Persey and I were orphans of the colonies. Both our lives had once been touched by the shipping lanes that took us and our parents across the globe. I had left India with my mother at the age of eighteen months. Persey and her sister were deposited with two spinster sisters who ran a sort of home for the abandoned children of the Empire somewhere on the south coast. She was two years old. Her sister a little older. Her father worked in Nigeria and her mother went back to join him.

We are in Persey's kitchen as usual. She is folding clothes into a laundry basket. I note she is much more domestic than me. I always seem to be sitting at a table with a cup of coffee. And when I'm at home alone I write. I don't do much folding or cooking or cleaning.

I can't remember a thing until we arrived at my grandmother's house,' I say. 'My grandmother standing at the door waiting for us. The tweed skirt. A blue butterfly brooch at her throat. Her white hair piled high on her head.

24

My mother told me she'd never had it cut. She could sit on it. Then me sitting under the table in the morning room and refusing to come out. Legs. Voices. My cousin Kerry bringing me a little rocking chair they'd bought me for a present. His head appearing under the table. A big toothy grin. I can't remember the ship or India.'

'I don't remember any of it,' Persey says. 'Not her leaving us there. Just waking in the morning and not knowing where I was. But that could have been any morning.'

'I'd been ill on the boat,' I say. 'They put me to bed in the old nursery in my grandmother's house. Called the doctor. I remember firelight on the ceiling and a silly man dancing round the bed to amuse me. I didn't feel ill.'

'Not sure I knew I even had a mother,' Persey says. She has stopped her folding and is holding a small woollen jumper which her mother had knitted for one of the children.

'Think I thought my ayah was my mother,' I say. 'She was the one who looked after me. And then this strange woman came and took me away. My mother tells me Jettie walked up and down the dock as we sailed away saying, 'Poor baba, poor baba.' She obviously didn't think my mother had a clue.'

'My sister said she wanted to run away but where to?' Persey muses.

'I kept running on the ship. Ran everywhere my mother said. My little feet pounding on the wooden deck. Never still for a moment. Think I was trying to run back to Jettie, to the only home I knew.'

'They were very nice to me at first,' Persey says. 'I was the youngest. They were always nice to the youngest one.'

She puts the jumper on the table and smooths it out. There is a picture. Fluffy clouds. Little lambs jumping in green fields.

25

'Then some golden-haired little dolly came along and I was out in the cold,' she says as she strokes the jumper. 'After that I was told to stop bothering them. I started to wet the bed – I must have been potty trained. They tied my wet nightdress round my neck.'

I think of her. A small dark child with button eyes. That penetrating look. I don't suppose she cried. I find I am angry. 'Christ,' I say, trying to divert my rage. 'Sounds like a scene from *Jane Eyre*. Did the other children cough a lot? Was there a vindictive clergyman involved?'

'Might as well have been. They used to come round at night and see we all had our hands outside the bedclothes. I don't know what they thought we'd get up to? We certainly didn't know.'

'But your sister. Didn't she look after you?'

'Hardly ever saw each other. Seemed to get used to it after a while. I suppose we thought this was what life was like.'

'Yes, well,' I say. 'I don't think I looked after my sister that well. Think I may be the reason they sent her away to boarding school. She was at school with me to begin with. I was horrible to her. Always dobbing her in. She said I told the housemistress she had broken some rule and she ended up knitting dusters.'

'What?'

'That was the punishment in our school. If you were reported for misdemeanours you got little bits of green paper called 'stripes' which you had to hand in at assembly. Stars and stripes. Stars were pink. If you got ten stripes you had to knit dusters. She said she only had nine and I'd told the housemistress she had ten and she had to knit dusters.'

'Did you?' Persey asks.

'Probably. I was always making up rules for her to break.'

'Better watch myself then.'

'What you mean?'

'Better not get into your "little sister" space.'

'What?' It takes me a moment to catch up.

'Looks like it could be fatal.'

I check to see she's not being entirely serious. 'Yes, right, see what you mean.'

'And I've never liked knitting,' she says, coming to sit at the table.

'I never had to do any.'

'No, you wouldn't. You were Miss Goody-Two-Shoes. I can't stand people who always play by the rules. I could never work out what they were?'

'Well, perhaps not school rules, but what about the rules that govern the universe. Aren't we busy looking for how to play by those?' I say.

We sit in silence for a while. The children are upstairs playing *Star Wars*. She takes a mouthful from a very cold cup of coffee, flinches and puts it down.

'Your sister. Didn't you like her?' Persey asks.

'Dunno, sometimes. They didn't give me a very good introduction.'

'How do you mean?'

'My mother told me she was going to London to get another baby and I asked her how she did that. She said she would choose one out of a box and she asked me what kind I'd like and I said I'd like a boy.'

'A boy, why?'

'The only other child I knew was my cousin Kerry and it was clear that boys were vastly superior to girls. He was forever telling me there were things that girls couldn't do.'

'Like what?'

'Pee standing up for a start. Climb trees. Play cricket. Anyway, I knew my mother wanted a boy. I'd heard her say so. And then she came back with a girl and I was outraged. Charlotte didn't stand a chance with me.'

'Didn't mind what I had,' says Persey almost to herself. 'My children kept wanting to get out early.'

I am still in full flow. 'She shouldn't have asked me what I wanted if she didn't mean to take any notice.'

'Daft the things they didn't tell children in those days,' she says.

'I tell Adam everything,' I continue. 'I have this book for kids about sex. Used to read to him quite often until one day he looked at me very hard and said, 'Do I need to know all this just yet?'

Persey laughs. 'Well, at least you got that conversation out the way.'

'Do you tell your kids things like that?'

'Bit difficult not to with animals all over the place.'

'We had animals. I didn't work it out until I was about to leave school and even then I sort of averted my eyes.'

'I suppose we only take things in when we're ready,' she says.

We sit. The game upstairs is hotting up. A lot of shooting and footsteps on the ceiling.

'What was she like,' she asks, 'your sister?'

'First she was a baby, which was very boring and then she was always trailing after me wanting to play. I didn't want to play with a baby and I certainly didn't want to play girls' games. I have this abiding memory of her standing under my tree trying to get me to come down and play with her. And then, of course, I sold all her dolls. Told her they were girls' toys and sold them at the gate. Don't think I even gave her the money. I wasn't very nice, was I?'

We sit in silence. I think of Charlotte. Our last conversation. She rang me in Ireland. I was getting ready to leave. She said she didn't know what to do with her life.

She wanted to die. I said not to be silly. Come over and help me pack. She said did I really think she was in a fit condition to pack? Hadn't I heard what she'd said? She wanted to die. I said something like, 'Well then, get on with it or shut up about it. What you think you're doing to mother?' And she said, what did I think I was doing to mother, leaving Ireland? And I put the phone down.

Back in Persey's kitchen I say, 'I think I'd be dead if she hadn't died first.'

'What?'

'I was about to leave Ireland. I remember feeling very transparent. Wafer-thin. I felt as though I was standing on top of a cliff in a high wind. At any moment the wind was going to blow me away. Then Charlotte came roaring past me and was gone, into the abyss. And I came back to myself and realised where I was. Her or me. That's what it felt like.'

'But you had a child, you had Adam.'

'Shows how close to the abyss I was.'

She picks up the jumper. Folds it and puts it on top of the pile of washing before getting up to put the basket on the stairs. It is getting dark outside. Her statue stands in the gloom like a gatekeeper.

'Do you like your sister?' I ask.

She turns and sits on the bottom step. Pauses. Perhaps, like me, she finds the answer difficult to locate. There are so many answers. So many times. So many feelings. I could see my sister sitting just like that on a stool in the sitting room. Telling me John, Adam's father, would never be able to marry me. There was no such thing as divorce in Ireland in those days. I remember wanting to kill her.

'She can be quite funny,' Persey says suddenly. 'Christened our mother "*Tinkling Bells*". We were on the ship on our way back to Nigeria. It was all cocktail parties and dinner with the captain and we'd hear her laughing. It was her cocktail laugh. Always across a crowded room. We lurked in the shadows avoiding the attentions of the other passengers. Dirty old men most of them. Don't think she wanted us around.'

'Do you think she missed you? Your mother. Do you think she minded?'

'Don't think they were supposed to miss us, were they? Had to choose between their husbands and their children. Everyone did it. Suppose she thought she was doing her duty or something like. Anyway I don't think she trusted him to be on his own all the time.'

'My father must have had an ayah,' I say. 'He never talked about her. Must have remembered her. He didn't leave India until he was eight, when they sent him back to school. Wrote about his early life when he went back to join the army. Endless stories about the war. Never talked about his childhood. Don't you think that's odd?'

'Perhaps he didn't remember?'

'He must have remembered. He was eight.'

'I don't remember a lot of my childhood,' she says. 'Not sure what's true or what we tell ourselves. Think we blank things.'

There is an enormous crash above our heads and then silence. We wait for the screams to follow. Then movement and more shooting. All's well.

'What do you think our children will think of us?' I ask.

'God knows. At least we're here.'

'And I've come back to my mother.'

'Think we all do that when push comes to shove,' she says. 'Especially when you have children. Sort of want to unravel things. Doesn't seem to work. My mother won't talk about anything except how I'm not doing the job properly. You'd think she'd know she abdicated that right years ago. Your Mum seems much more human.'

'She likes her horses. She's great with Adam. She reads him stories like she used to read to me. She always read to us. My head has always been full of stories.'

'Sounds like heaven to me. Can't see what the problem is.'

'I think she sort of likes me, but I know it's my brother who she really loves. And Charlotte. She liked Charlotte. Always said she had more fun with her. Think they were quite alike in many ways. Always scrapping. We never fight. Not her and me. Think she finds me a bit daunting.'

'But you came back,' she says.

'Couldn't think of where else to go.'

---

*Today in the mosque I was sent to pray with the women for my second attendance. Kicked up a fuss as I always normally pray with the men (maybe I have already told you that I think I may be he first woman in Islam to pray in the men-only mosques). Anyway, the women made such a fuss of me during the sermon that a friendly old man popped into our section and suggested it was time I left. They all came up to me (at least a good many did) when prayers were finished and wanted to know where I came from. From England, I said, and that seemed to silence them. NO GOOD GOVERNMENT they said. We are not much respected here.*

---

# THE EMPEROR

*Alex [sitting on a tiger skin]: Remember you, you old bugger. Lovely winter's morning. Just after a fall of rain. The jungle steep above me. Bright and clear in the winter sun. Sitting on the slope waiting for a good chital stag. So much in love with the landscape I didn't care much if I saw one or not. Then I heard you. A long swelling moan, moving up through the valley like a summer flood. The moment when you came out of the undergrowth and saw me. Seeing you gather yourself. Flight or attack. Impossible to know. Already in my sights. The kick of the gun against my shoulder. Your body falling. The crash as you hit the ground and I waited... to see if you were really dead or about to get up and finish me off. You or me. Think you may have got the best deal in the long run...*

*MISSING*

I am standing on a station platform. Legs everywhere. We are here to meet my father. He is coming home. I can't remember him but my mother tells me he has a broken nose and I imagine something like a squashed tomato on his face. There is a lot of noise and I'm frightened. The train arrives. Steam and wheels and monstrous sounds. I am screaming. My mother picks me up.

I don't remember seeing him at the station. I see him standing in the hall at my grandmother's house. He says something to me. I hold on to my mother's skirt. I don't know this man. His nose looks nothing like a squashed tomato. Is she sure this is my father? How does she know? He smells like every other man I know. Tobacco and damp tweed. He could be anyone.

We had left my father behind in India. That's what she

told me. Later I understood that he administered a district as the country moved towards independence in 1947. Things he saw then shocked him much more than anything he had seen in the war. Trains full of bodies. Men he'd fought with, could have died with, melting into the night because it was no longer safe for them to be seen talking to him. He probably didn't know what he was doing here either.

'They never talked about anything but India,' I say. 'I was quite sure we were all in the wrong place now we were "home".'

This time we are sitting in the back room of my cottage. The wind is lifting the makeshift draught excluder I have fixed to the door. We sit close to the quietly hissing Rayburn with our obligatory cups of coffee.

'My father had me named by a local medicine man long before I was christened,' Persey says. 'I have a name that sounds something like Oozo Amaka. I think it means *Your coming is good.*'

I think of her, a tiny bundle being welcomed into the world. The sounds of the African night. Leaves cracking after a day of rain. Firelight. Drums. The women dancing. The medicine man calling her name, alerting the ancestors to her arrival.

'My mother called me Linda,' she adds. 'Both my sister and I changed our names as soon as we grew up. Names are funny things aren't they?'

'So why Persephone?' I ask.

'Dunno really. I think I liked the idea of her disappearing into the underworld with Hades and giving her mother grief. Making her know that if she wanted her daughter back she had to plead for her.'

'In the book of Greek myths my mother read to me,' I say. 'There was a picture of Hades breaking out of the earth in a chariot drawn by two black horses, coming to carry her off. Rather fancied him myself.'

'David was very good-looking when he was young,' she says absently. 'Don't think my mother approved.'

We sit again for a while. A cat comes up and glares at us for stealing his place by the fire. I have two cats, both brought from Ireland. A grey and white tom called W.B. after the Irish poet W.B.Yeats, and a beautiful Siamese Tabby Point appropriately named Maude Gonne, Yeats' great love and long-time muse, and duly adored by W.B. We make room.

'What do you think your father was doing when he gave you to the medicine man?' I ask as the cat settles.

'Probably thought it was a way of making me safe,' says Persey.

'You don't think he thought you were one of his ancestors?'

'Perhaps he did. Nice idea. Coming back to your family. But then we don't believe in that sort of thing. We Christians!'

'Wasn't always the case,' I say. 'Think it was only ruled out as an idea because the Catholic Church couldn't cope with it. Cathars believed in it.'

'Who?'

I had been reading my sister's books. There was a lot about reincarnation in them. In particular there was a book, *We Are One Another*, by an NHS psychiatrist, Arthur Guirdham. He writes about a patient who seemed to have memories of being burned as a Cathar heretic in 13th century France and explores the possibility of group incarnations. I am rather taken with the idea.

'Early Christian sect. Very big in the Languedoc and Northern Italy in the Middle Ages. Sound rather a good lot to me. Believed in living a simple life. Thought the worldly power and pomp of the Catholic Church was the work of the Devil.

'That wouldn't go down too well I suppose,' says Persey.

'Thing that interests me most is that they treated women as equals. They had women priests.'

'Definitely ripe for burning then.'

'*Parfait* they were called. Men and women. As long as you had fulfilled all your family obligations you could become a 'Parfait'. Give up sex. Stop eating meat. Wander about giving people consolation. No hierarchy. No churches. Services took place in people's houses or in the open. They were supported by the local aristocracy as well as the ordinary people. A whole society. Wiped out by the end of 13th century.'

'I've never heard of them.'

'Me neither. Really annoyed when I found out about them. Edited out of history.'

'And they believed in reincarnation?'

'They didn't like the idea of coming back. The aim was to be so pure that you didn't have to. But yes, they believed.'

'Bit like the Hindus and the Buddhists...

'And your medicine man...'

'So, what do you think?'

'Makes as much sense as anything else,' I say.

'I'd like to come back to see my children,' Persey says, bending to stroke the cat who promptly moves off.

I think about my sister reading these books. Of her journey through the world looking for meaning, for the place where she felt she belonged. She used to say she was looking for her tribe.

'Wonder if Charlotte bailed out because she thought she might have better luck in her next life,' I say.

35

'Not sure you're supposed to commit suicide, are you?' says Persey. 'Thought you had to stay with what you got?'

'She told my brother and sister-in-law she would like them to be her parents.'

We sit for a while. The wind humming in the chimney. 'Come to think of it my father wrote a book about it,' I say.

'About what?'

'About reincarnation.'

'Really?'

'Not a very good book. His hero reincarnates through periods of Indian history serving all the great leaders Alexander, Akbar… and falling in love with the same two women with various levels of success. All very romantic but not very well-written. Odd – he could write, but this one seems to have escaped him.'

'Sounds rather interesting. Do you think he believed it?'

'Never asked him. Wasn't speaking to him. Think it was his fantasy life – being the hero. In the book he had a spiritual teacher who went with him, kept his mind on higher things. A sort of quest I suppose. Don't know what he believed.'

'He's not turned up again then?' Persey asks.

'What?'

'Your father, has he come back?'

'God, I hope not.'

'Isn't that the implication?'

'Fought like cat and dog when I was growing up,' I say. 'Spent large parts of his life in the airing cupboard with a bottle of whiskey. Don't think that would be much fun.'

I glance towards the cupboard under the stairs. Big enough. I must make sure it isn't inhabited.

'You'll have a lot to sort out then,' she says.

That night lying in bed, with Adam curled up beside me, I think about my father. The fights. The years of rage. Him teasing me mercilessly. Not sure he knew what else to do with children. He teased my sister too but she didn't seem to mind. But then there were good things. A friend who used to come to stay in the holidays said he was a wonderful father. She said he treated us like small adults. Always doing things with us.

I am about four. He's bought us a pony in the market. A round little Dartmoor pony called Cocoa. He puts me on it. Smacks the pony's bottom. We fly off across the field. 'Hold on with your knees.' he shouts after me. 'Pull on your right rein.' I am holding onto the mane so tight I can't pull on anything. 'Point him towards the hedge.' The hedge appears. The pony stops. I go straight over its head. I sit on the ground and wail. My father arrives, grabs the pony by the bridle and kicks it. I scream at him for doing that. He gets me back on the pony and tells me that's what you have to do. That's a rule for life. 'Get back on the bloody horse and stop bellyaching.' I am a nervous child but I've already got the message about being a hero and the boy hasn't arrived yet.

The story was much the same with the bicycle. I don't remember training wheels. Perhaps they didn't have them then. Just my father putting me on and giving me a shove. Didn't take long to get the hang of it. And then I was off. All round the country lanes. Out on adventures with anyone who had a bicycle. Long afternoons in the barn with boys from the village discussing how to build a bike from an old frame we'd found in a ditch.

He got me my first gun when I was six. An air rifle. Didn't seem to be very lethal but I learnt to aim. To hold the gun into my shoulder and follow the flight of a bird. Later, when I'd graduated to a .410 shotgun, when I was about ten, he would run holding an old football over his head and I was supposed to shoot that. Considering our ongoing relationship, it was lucky I didn't shoot him.

Tennis. Long hours on a friend's tennis court patting the ball back and forth. 'Keep your eye on the ball.' He was always shouting at me. 'Keep your eye on the ball and follow through.' Another aphorism for how to live your life?

And films. My mother didn't like going to the cinema so he took me. We went twice a week. Once to the Odeon. Once to the fleapit by the station. I must have seen every war film, every Western. I always walked out playing the hero, not the heroine. The women in the films we saw all seemed to be left behind or made to change into a dress so the men would like them. That didn't seem to me to be much of a deal. So I created a fantasy life where I was a hero with a boy's name. All my friends had to do the same. I don't remember us going to the more romantic films but perhaps we did. I do remember him taking mother to *The Million Pound Note,* a film starring Gregory Peck, and feeling absolute outrage. Going to the cinema was my domain and I had been in love with Gregory Peck ever since I'd seen *Captain Hornblower.* I don't think I spoke to my father for a week.

As I grew up, there were some really funny moments. Like the day when a boyfriend took me out in the old London taxi he had as his form of transport. We came back late that night. The boyfriend got out of the driver's seat and joined me in the back. There was some heavy petting. Nothing more. Mother had gone to bed. Father was up. Next morning he remarked to my mother. 'I didn't know what to do. Peppy was kissing the taxi driver. Should I have done something?' My mother assured him not.

Much later, when my sister and I were both in our twenties, there was a moment in the kitchen when he said we mustn't sleep with anyone before we got married because 'men didn't like spoiled goods.' We both roared with laughter and said he was a little late with that advice. I don't think he really knew what to do with daughters.

So no, on reflection, he wasn't the worst father in the world. But we fought. Some of it was to do with the arrival of my brother and the fact that I lost my place as his surrogate son. Some of it just because of the way we were. We argued about everything. I had to be right of course. I remember coming downstairs in the night clutching a copy of the *Encyclopaedia Britannica*, just to win an argument he had probably already forgotten about.

The rest had to do with the fact that he had a long-term romance with a woman in the town which drove my mother to distraction. For years we never sat down to a meal without some mention of 'the bitch'. And I was quite sure I knew who was in the right there. Well, I did then.

He had a kind of nervous breakdown when he was about fifty-five and retired to the airing cupboard, which was really a small room with a window and the immersion heater. Here he read romantic historical novels by Georgette Heyer and drank whiskey. The rest of the time he sat in front of the television in the sitting room dressed in an old mac and a cap. Except when he was very ill, he didn't sleep in a bed for the last ten years of his life.

No one knew quite what all this was about. My brother says it was triggered by an attack of angina one day out hunting and he wouldn't go to bed in case he died. Charlotte, who was much more emotionally aware than I was, said it was the war. She used to hear him shouting in the night. Of course no one bothered about post-traumatic stress in those days and he was a professional soldier, a hero, a legend in the regiment. He couldn't possibly have admitted to being damaged by war. I think my mother called in a psychiatrist at some point to try and deal with his drinking but father soon saw him off. And me? I took it as a form of betrayal. Him not being there for me. I suppose death in war was OK. Death in peacetime was an entirely different matter.

When mother moved from the house with the airing cupboard to a wonderful 14th century farmhouse with none, he used to sit by a storage radiator in the sitting room. She didn't even bother to provide him with a bedroom as he hadn't been to bed for so long. Charlotte and I could hear him downstairs in the night tapping his pipe out on the chimney breast and snoring on the sofa. One night the snoring stopped and we consulted each other through the wall between our bedrooms. Had he died? Should one of us go down and check? And then the snoring started up again.

At one point he became very ill and had to be put into a bed. The bed was brought into the sitting room as there was no bedroom for him. Mother stayed down most nights to attend to him and when she wasn't there he sometimes called for me to bring him a bottle to pee in. A very odd duty for a daughter who had hardly spoken to him for years. After a month or so my mother was so sure he was going to die that she took his clothes to a jumble sale. Then one day she came home from hunting to find him standing by the fireplace demanding to know where his trousers were and she had to go out and buy him some new ones.

The last time I saw him alive he was sitting by the storage heater. Whiskey in one hand, Georgette Heyer in the other. Being ignored by all of us. I don't think we said anything of much importance. I was on my way to Ireland. He was on his way to death and I think he knew it. I hadn't been in Ireland for more than a week when my mother rang to tell me. She'd gone out on the farm to feed the sheep. Come back to find him with his face on the storage heater. Book on the floor. He had slipped away while she was out.

My response was to ask if she wanted me to come home for the funeral. That's how disconnected we'd become.

No, he hadn't been a bad father, just a damaged one. A man who had left his childhood in India when he was eight-years-old. Been transported on a ship that was in danger of being sunk by German U-boats – this was during the First World War – and deposited at a prep school in England where his housemaster took him behind the gym to teach him how to box so that he could look after himself. When his father died he was at public school and hadn't seen him for two years. His father was an engineer in India and only came home on long leave every three years. He had died of smallpox, having neglected to have his vaccination on his last visit to England. In my mind I imagine my father, a boy of fourteen, being called to the headmaster's study to be told the news. I have a feeling he probably just went back to what he was doing at the time. You weren't supposed to show any emotion.

Not that he didn't show emotion when I knew him. Our house was a cauldron of emotion from morning 'til night. My brother described it as like living in a war zone. When I was about six I remember being terrified when my mother locked him out one evening and he tried to climb in through my bedroom window. Mostly I stayed upstairs during the rows, telling myself my brother needed looking after. Charlotte was the one who went down to try and stop them. One Christmas, when we were well into our teens, they were roaring round the house shouting at each other. Father went into the bedroom where he never slept and let off a gun. I think he wanted mother to think he'd shot himself. And she did, for a moment. Happy times.

I remembered the smell of him. Tweed and whiskey. Dubbin for waterproofing the boots. Hair oil and shaving cream and Tabasco sauce. Him calling for things he thought the cleaning woman had lost. Calling to the dogs. The smell of dogs. The smell of horses. The smell of the oil he used to clean the guns. Guns. We all grew up with guns. 'Never, never let your gun, pointed be at anyone.' Another aphorism. He forgot to tell Charlotte not to point it at herself.

---

*In fact I used to pray with the women in the mosque of Ali in Istanbul (and with the men before the Altar rail in the Blue Mosque there) but in Iran I have always prayed with the men until today simply because of going into the men only mosques which they don't have, as such, in any of the other countries I have visited except Afghanistan and Kashmir. It was fun – gave the usual spiel about praying with men elsewhere, and they said they didn't give a fig what I did elsewhere – was in Kerman now and did what they said! In fact it is great to be with the women periodically. We kiss each other and you can smile from your heart without having to be aware of the fact that if you smile too much for too long you are behaving like a whore – which I hope I NEVER DO!! There are snow covered mountains all around here, and bits of desert stretching up to the town. The dates, of course, are excellent and very cheap, so pig myself on them!*

---

# THE HIEROPHANT

*Today*
*There were rabbits*
*In the ruins*
*Of the big house*
*And a fox stalked*
*The sunken road*
*Through the bones*
*Of the chestnut wood*

*Men*
*Cannon felled*
*To keep the stones standing*
*Trees*
*Cut*
*To fence the cattle*
*Fattening in the valley*

*ELMSTEAD 1978*

Reincarnation. Persey and I weren't going to leave that one alone. Far too good a device for speculation. Besides, like my father, I was on a quest. Ever since arriving on my hill I had been writing about my early life, trying to work out why I had such huge emotional responses to things, what I was frightened of. Apart from the separation from my ayah and living in a family war zone I had a very privileged childhood. Horses, private education, endless freedom.

My mother didn't know where I was until I came home for tea. And she read to me. Every night for at least an hour. Beatrix Potter, *Wind in the Willows, The Lion, the Witch and the Wardrobe, Ring of Bright Water, Black Beauty, King Solomon's Mines, Treasure Island, Captain Hornblower,* Greek myths, Norse myths. It was Captain

43

Hornblower that really grabbed my imagination. For years I ran a fantasy life in which I was the captain of a three-masted ship of the line, fighting the Spanish and bringing back the spoils. One of the apple trees in our orchard was my ship and the cornfield over the hedge the sea on which I sailed.

Perhaps I just thought my life should read like a good book and was annoyed when it wouldn't follow the rules? But what if there were more lives? What if the plot was more intricate and longer than I had ever imagined? What if I my father was right when he wrote about his hero travelling through history? What if the answers lay just out of sight in other lives? Immediately I felt the weight lift.

You could say that I wasn't really dealing with the loss of my sister but, even before considering reincarnation, I had a sense in which she was just on yet another of her wild adventures and I would catch up with her someday. I had always envied her capacity to take off into the unknown, usually on her own. I have always been very good at having adventures in my head, but I have never been quite so brave in real life. And now, her books were leading me somewhere.

Persey and I returned to the charts, adding reincarnation as a possible ingredient. What could they tell us about what we brought with us? Charts and hand reading. Yes, Charlotte had a book about that as well.

Persey's hand was small and soft, if a bit calloused from looking after the animals, and very open-hearted as I remember it. Mine is a maze of lines, but interesting to read. I have a good long life line – well, that is beginning to prove itself. A head line with a 'writer's fork' – good for my purposes. A line of fate which runs up to the finger of Saturn – a life which is already laid out for me, a life full of lessons. And an emotional line which explains a lot of my difficulties with relationships. It is forked. One branch goes up to meet the finger of Jupiter, the other goes straight across my hand. This is the hand of a fanatic. Of someone who always wants to be right, to be in possession of the one and only truth. I would have made a very effective inquisitor. To maintain a good relationship you need a line that stops on the mound under the index finger. This shows a capacity to allow other people to be themselves. Persey had this line.

Persey's reading of my hand included the fact that I have uncountable lines on the mound of Venus. She said again, that I was born to know every person on the planet. Living in isolation up a hill was not my natural habitat. My left hand is very similar. This is the hand you supposedly bring with you from previous lives. She said she thought I'd exhausted myself in a previous life and perhaps I needed a rest before becoming myself again. She had decided that this was what our hands and our charts were about. Not who we were, but who we were going to become. A sort of road map for keeping your mind on the task.

*'Who are you going to become?'*

That rang a bell. I am sitting in a doctor's surgery in Dublin, unmarried and about to become a mother. The doctor takes this in, looks out of the window and asks me, just that question. 'And who are you going to become?'

To begin with I took this as an existential question. I said I thought I was going to be the person I always had been. Did becoming a mother turn you into someone else? And then I realised, of course, that he wanted to know who I was going to marry. I might have engaged him on the question of whether the act of getting married might make similar demands on my identity but I decided to leave the surgery and find another doctor.

This time I told the doctor I was married, invented a

wedding date and temporarily took on the name of the father of the child. We couldn't actually marry because we were living in Holy Catholic Ireland and divorce was not yet part of the deal.

This led to all sorts of other complications. The day in the doctor's waiting room when I sat there reminding myself of my 'married' name only to find that when the receptionist came in and announced it, two of us went for the door. Had she invented her name as well, I wondered?

I was booked into a private nursing home run by nuns. What better place to hide who I was? My mother came over for the birth. The child was born and we decided to call him Adam. But then came the moment when he had to be registered. I was having a leisurely bath when a nun appeared and said she was going to register the births and had she got the baby's names right?

'Oh, no,' I say in alarm, thinking both Adam and I would be forever trapped in our false identities. 'We want to do that. His father and I.'

'But we always do the registration,' she insists. She already had the pad and pencil in her hand.

'No, no,' I say again, feeling very exposed, lying as I was stark naked in the presence of a very well-covered nun. 'It is a very personal matter, we want to do that ourselves.'

Eventually she backed out defeated and John and I went to the registrar together. But that was not the end of it. I wanted my son to have my surname as John and I were not married and I had given birth to him. But, no, said the registrar, his father was present so he must have his father's name. I had a vague notion that you could give a child any surname you liked but he assured me this was not the case.

Luckily, John knew people in high places and we went home and he rang the Chief Registrar, who said there was no rule to say that if the father was present the child had to have his surname. Only that if he wasn't present, and hadn't signed the form and was not married to the mother, then the child could not be given his name in his absence. Adam got my name.

Before that there was the wonderful moment in the nursing home when my mother turned up rather late in the day saying, 'I'm so sorry, darling, sorry I'm late. I just couldn't remember who you were.'

Being myself was obviously a much more complicated issue than I had first supposed.

Back in the kitchen Persey asks, 'What was your sister's hand like?'

I think about it. 'She had a very strange head line which plunged down her hand into the mound of the moon.'

Persey had the book open. 'Says here she lived too much in her imagination, not at all grounded. But clever. Too insightful perhaps. Not enough protection from the horrors of the world.'

'Does it suggest suicide?' I ask.

'Not directly. But then it says here it is illegal to predict death.'

We pause for a while looking at an illustration of a big square hand with short defined lines. A very practical hand with a long strong life line.

'What was her life line like?' asks Persey.

'Don't remember a break in it,' I say. 'Perhaps a few marks. But nothing to suggest...'

'Doesn't always mean anything... you remember the vicar?' says Persey with a wicked look in her dark eyes.

We both laugh. We had offered our services at the village fête as fortune tellers. We weren't getting many takers to begin with because the vicar – a very tall man who always wore a black cloak and had been christened

'Dracula' by the children – stood in front of our table telling the passers-by that we were doing the work of the devil.

We let him carry on for a bit and then I say, 'Come over here and have your hand read, then you can tell us whether what we're doing is any more dangerous than the stories you tell.'

After a bit more persuasion, and the presence of a small crowd, he agrees. I turn over his right hand and see that his lifeline is alarmingly short. He must have been about fifty at the time.

I look up at him and say, 'You shouldn't be alive, according to this. Are you sure you're not dead?' Some laughter from the crowd and both of us gazing at his hand in bemusement.

'What were you doing in your twenties?' Persey asks him.

'Matter of fact I was in the army. Came out to join the church.'

'Looks to me if you hadn't made that career change you would have been killed,' she says, taking his hand from me and holding it out for others to see. 'Look, look at this life line. It stops about an inch from the top.'

People crowd round to look. She gives him his hand back. 'God clearly wanted you for something else. God saved your life.'

He couldn't argue with that and wandered off looking hard at his palm. We hadn't asked to see his left hand so didn't get round to speculating about what he'd done in his past life. Perhaps that was enough for one day.

'That was a bit odd,' says Persey. 'We'll have to do a survey. See if that's the mark of the holy man.'

'Or a vampire,' I say under my breath.

We got quite a few takers after that.

*Had a splendid time in Lahore where I spent three days and got to see the Fort, the big mosque beside it (which has had all the embellishments removed over the past 100 or 150 years) and generally got around a lot. Didn't see the museum there as it was closed, but probably like some of the stuff I saw in the museum in Peshawar, where I also spent three days before going to Kashmir. Made great friends with 5 or 6 year old hunchbacked boy in Lahore. He took ages, at least about a day, to approach me, and after that we were inseparable pals whenever I went to the pavement chai stall his father owned until the day I left, when he ignored me!!*

# THE LOVERS

*It is cold again*
*Today*
*But there is a smell*
*Of summer coming*
*Yesterday*
*There was sun*
*And the dark earth*
*Remembers*

*ELMSTEAD 1978*

So here I was with Persephone, the Queen of the Underworld who was only allowed to return to the world for six months of the year when her mother begged for her return. And here she was with Penelope the woman who wove, waiting for her husband to come back from the wars.

Persey continued to plan her escape. I stayed home each day and wrote and unpicked and wrote again, just like Penelope with her weaving, although contrary to the story there were no suitors camped outside my door. I was writing a book called *And In Another Kingdom Penelope Sat Weaving,* which was the beginning of an exploration of my relationship with my sister, a way of giving her a voice. Persey was doing the illustrations which reflected her own journey. Moves on a chessboard.

Then, one day, when I was down at my mother's farm, an old school friend arrived out of the blue. She was an artist, quite a rebel during our school days, and now living in the States. I found her standing outside the gate one afternoon.

We walked. We talked. I was probably more honest with her about my strange obsessions than I might otherwise have been. She suggested I go to a consciousness raising course which she said had done her a lot of good, got her out of a hole when she broke up with her husband. It was called *est* and had grown out of the self-motivating salesman culture of the time. There was a recruitment event in London in the not too distant future.

A messenger at my gate. I took it as a sign from the gods.

I was not comfortable leaving my hill and its daily rituals, but this seemed important. I arranged for Adam to stay with my brother's family and organised everything meticulously before I went. Not wanting to waste the train ticket I found a film that I really wanted to see, *Meetings With Remarkable Men* devised and directed by Peter Brook, a theatre director who was one of my heroes. Based on an autobiography of the same name, it tells the story of Gurdjieff's spiritual awakening. Another portent perhaps?

Film over, I still had plenty of time on my hands and wandered off to the British Museum, which was very close to where I'd worked before going to Ireland. Even so I arrived at the preliminary meeting in the hotel hours before anyone else and sat waiting in the corner of the foyer trying to look like a writer observing humanity for a new novel.

Who was going to care about that for god's sake? Who the hell was going to notice me? But there was another lost soul, also early, also trying not to look conspicuous. *What a nice looking man,* I thought. Older than me, shorter, lots of dark hair, a kind of intensity that was interesting. What was he doing here?

Eventually someone arrived with a clipboard and a jug of coffee and we both made for the table and realised we were waiting for the same meeting. We chatted about nothing in particular. Other people arrived. We went into the meeting and got separated in the general mêlée.

The course sounded like something that might help. I

was desperate for some kind of shift and this was all about self-empowerment. That couldn't be a bad thing, I thought. And the signs from the Tarot had been encouraging. Pictures of ships and people preparing for new journeys. *The Fool* stepping off a cliff. I signed up for the course and took off for the train station and my journey home.

I was mounting the steps at my destination when a voice behind me said, 'What's a nice girl like you doing in a place like this?' or something to that effect. And there he was. Two steps below me. The man from the meeting.

He was Australian. An artist. And had brought his family to England, thinking the old country would live up to expectations delivered in jolly black and white films with nice men in tweeds and ties and ladies who made cakes and waited for their men to come home. They were living only a few miles away. His name was William.

I had my car at the station. I gave him a lift home. He smiled and touched my face as we said goodbye. I remember thinking, *I must not fall in love with this man.* But of course I did.

So now I had another Odysseus to wait for and he... well, to be quite honest, we were both a little mad. His marriage was in trouble. His wife was having an affair with one of their friends who had also been to *est*. William was finding it difficult to cope. Had been told he needed to go on the course 'to sort himself out'. And me? I would have followed anyone out of my isolation, anyone who could see me.

William and I had a very odd relationship. He was in love with me for a while. I was in love with him for a lot longer. But then by this time I wasn't used to a man about the house. My profession was in waiting.

We were never quite sure how I got pregnant. We never seemed to reach a satisfactory conclusion. He was always haunted by guilt and the fact that I don't think he ever really fell out of love with his wife. We got into bed a couple of times but nothing much happened. We never really connected on any level, but somehow I got pregnant. A situation which resulted in legendary status for William with women refusing to sit in a chair he'd recently vacated, just in case.

I didn't know quite how I was going to tell my mother, but when I did I assured William she would make her feelings known. We went down to the farm one morning and William asked her, politely, how the lambing was going?

'Oh,' she said, setting her jaw in a very characteristic manner, 'very well considering. There are some rather early lambs, the ram got out.'

He had been told.

Everyone seemed to take it very well. We were all of an artistic bent and life was supposed to be about everyone accepting everyone else and respecting their journey through life, and other such claptrap. Anyway I was pregnant and I wasn't going to do anything about it, so on we went. More walks round the hill. More Tarot readings with Persey and a certain amount of bemusement as neither of us had predicted this!

And then William went back to Australia to wrap up the life they had left behind and his wife and children, at my suggestion, moved to a house not one hundred yards down the road. It was the house my brother had lived in, until they moved to take over our mother's farm. The house from which my sister had walked out into the night and shot herself. This was becoming like the plot of a terrible modern novel.

I have a letter from him from that time – one of two I had from him over the three years. He is in Australia. He is going to come back. But am I Circe, the enchantress who kept Odysseus away from home, or Penelope, the faithful wife? His real-life wife is living in a house down the road. I am inhabiting a story entirely of my own making.

Anyway, this is the letter:

*Dear Peppy,*

*Strange, this is the first time that I have written to you. I have your letters (2). I would have written sooner except I had little to say except I love you. I arrived here with tremendous power and a lust for life – I felt transformed into a new being. I'm calming down a bit now, all that booze and partying, champagne around swimming pools and being recognised as an identity, regaining what I had lost in England. A great feeling of being alive in this universe and enjoying every moment.*

*Peppy, I like being with you and miss your winning smile and the tallness of you. It's going to be okay. I'll be back in three weeks. I'm missing that lovely spring weather. The countryside is burnt out here, bleached. I'm working very hard, selling off my past. My six weeks of glory. My time. Give my love to Adam and let him know that I am upside down beneath his feet,*

*All my love*
*William.*

What I hadn't realised was that when he came back and was living just down the road everything became much more difficult. I would watch for him coming and going from the house, but his visits became very sparse. There was one occasion when the waiting got too much for me and I marched into the house demanding his attendance. They had friends round for lunch, but that wasn't going to deter me. He came out. I sat on the wall by the church and said something had to happen. He said he had been very much in love with me at the beginning, but now he needed to sort his marriage out. Persey warned me against being a 'bunny boiler' and I tried to behave myself. It was very hard.

On another occasion – may have been earlier – there was a meeting. Me, William, the wife and the lover, all of us now *est* graduates and stuffed with aphorisms about how to handle life and relationships. I was informed that I was being too possessive and must proceed into the future as though William had died. Seemed a bit extreme to me, especially as the lover appeared to have free access to the house and not to have to think that anyone was dead.

Anyway, I was pregnant. The summer was hot and dusty. I felt well. I wrote. I walked the hill. Every day I passed the place where my sister had died. Every day I passed his house. William had chosen an upstairs room as his studio. Occasionally I would see him sitting at the window. Sometimes he saw me and waved. Mostly he didn't. Occasionally he showed me his paintings. Strange abstract watercolours which didn't tell me anything.

Autumn came. The corn was cut. The hedges filled with berries. The child was slow in arriving but on my last check up the doctor disturbed something and I started going into labour not long afterwards. I went down the road to enquire whether William wanted to be present at the birth. His reply was to say he hadn't seen any of his other children born, he wasn't going to start now. So off I went on my own with my mother riding shotgun.

I lay in the ward with several first-time mothers and the contractions were coming fast and furious. Shit, I had forgotten this bit, and wasn't keeping quiet about it. They moved me out of the ward before I terrified all the others.

Took me straight to the delivery ward. The baby wasn't slow to arrive although I did indulge in gas and air and was informed that half the hospital could hear me.

With Adam I hadn't been able to feed him straightaway, but I was determined to feed this baby the minute he arrived. I tried. He looked at me. 'I have only just been born, do you mind, I need a rest.' He lay there with a shock of red hair. William's first remark was, 'That can't be mine, must be the milkman's.' I pointed out that the milkman was a woman and anyway my father had red hair. In all other respects he is very like his father.

This time I didn't have to tussle with the registrar. William didn't turn up to put his name on the certificate so his son was automatically given my surname. I didn't know quite what to do next.

I hadn't had Adam christened mainly because I didn't believe in Holy Catholic Ireland or any kind of god at the time. But this time I wanted a way of acknowledging young William's arrival. A way of making him visible in this strange, mythical landscape we seemed to inhabit. Most of all I wanted to honour my next-door neighbour who had seen me through some very bleak times, before I even met Persey.

Jackie was definitely not invisible. She arrived on my doorstep almost the first morning I moved in. She was about twenty-five at the time, thin and fierce, with short dark hair streaked with green and pink and cripple boots dyed to match. She had been half-paralysed as a result of falling on a table leg during a fight with her husband – a very mild man as far as I could tell – but she wasn't going to lie down and die. They still lived together and had a daughter and a crowd of colourful relations who lived a couple of miles away.

In the early days Jackie and I used to sit and talk all

morning round my Rayburn, usually both at once. Her husband said he never knew how we heard what the other one was saying but it seemed to work. On the day I went into labour she was out riding a small, grey pony someone lent to her and arrived at a gallop as I was getting into my mother's car. I asked her to be a godmother.

At first this caused some minor problems. The vicar – 'Dracula' – arrived to make arrangements and said he didn't think he could accept her as a godparent as she was not of 'the true faith'. I asked him what that meant since she declared herself a Christian. He said she was Roman Catholic and this apparently was not allowed.

'But both the fathers of my children are Catholic, what are you saying?' I protested.

He went away none too convinced but the woman who delivered the milk soon put him right. She had watched over us for at least two years at that stage and wasn't going to have him upsetting 'her girls'. So Jackie and her husband become godparents along with my brother and an absent sister from William's first marriage (also a Catholic).

He was named after his father 'William Thomas' and 'Eliot' because it was George Eliot's anniversary and I wanted a literary reference. He was a good eater and I called him 'the hungry bundle' which resulted in him being called 'Bun' throughout his childhood. I will use that name for the time being so that there is no confusion with his father.

In normal circumstances I might not have persisted with the christening but we seemed to have fallen rather short on ritual. I wasn't married. Adam wasn't christened. My sister hadn't been buried. We had had her cremated and collected the ashes, but no one had done anything since. She was tucked away in the drinks' cupboard in my mother's – now my brother's – house where the Christmas decorations were also stored. The result was a Christmas ritual in which the children would go looking for the decorations and emerge with the urn demanding to know what it was. 'That's your Aunty Charlotte. Put her back,' was the standard response.

So, as well as christening my younger son, I decided it was time to bury my sister. Charlotte now has a small plaque in the churchyard at the top of the hill where she died and young William has his name on a scroll in the church. His father was not at the christening.

---

*When I was in Pakistan I wrote and told Peppy how I loved Quetta. The Tonga drivers are nuts – they will gallop their horses down the hard roads like maniacs. I suppose they did it there in your day too. I was given a camel ride in a camel cart there. My hotel was excellent (again Moslem only). I can't stand "hippy hotels" where the tourists keep to themselves and smoke far too much hash, with little or no idea how to smoke it in most cases. They charged me something like 50p a night for the first two nights I was there and the third night was free, and when I got back from the days wanderings at around 10pm they all sat up and chatted in excellent English, laid on chai and milk drinks etc..*

---

# THE CHARIOT

*I thought you were my life. I thought I had to wait. I thought I had no choice. Every morning waking to the sounds of the household stirring round me. Every day walking to the cliff top and watching. Hoping I'd see your sail on the horizon coming home to the house I kept for you. But nothing changed. The sea was always empty. And I'd go back into the house and weave new colours into the cloth and wait again.*

*TROJAN WHORES*

Sometime after Bun was born, William and his family moved away from the hill to set up a gallery in Canterbury and I was involved in another kind of waiting – watching again for his car, hoping they'd find they couldn't stand each other after all.

Persey, on the other hand, was on the move. She decided she'd had enough of her marriage. She sent her husband away, sold the house and moved closer to me. She also joined a dating agency. She didn't like hanging around, our Persey.

The result was a large and determined bloke called Desmond who started moving heavy pieces of furniture into her new house as a sign of commitment. She found these rather oppressive and I spent many happy hours helping her move them out to the garage, both of us giggling helplessly. She had also added a Lassie type dog to the menagerie, which was rather overbred and very nervous. Her old dog had died.

And now I am restless. I want to get away from this hill. Find another place to be. We settle on Greece.

First we thought of Corfu. We had both read *My Family and Other Animals* by Gerald Durrell and had visions of our children playing with lizards and swimming with dolphins.

We booked a car and a villa in the hills above Corfu Town and took Bun with us.

The car was nearly our downfall. I drove and found it difficult to assess where the body of the car was as I was not used to a left-hand drive. I know Persey thought she was going to end her days at the bottom of any number of deep ravines as we wound our way round the mountain roads. With a little drink taken I also had a tendency to scrape the parked cars on the right-hand side of the road.

One dark night coming out of Corfu Town after supper I started hearing strange banging sounds. I thought at first it was someone putting out the bins – a very unlikely occupation in Greece – but then voices were added to the mix. Rather angry voices, I thought.

'You're hitting all the cars down this side of the road,' says Persey.

'Oh god,' I say, slowing down. 'I'd better stop and apologise.'

'No, no, for god's sake! Do you want to get us killed?'

At the time importing a car into Greece cost more than the price of a house. We drove off into the night and luckily no one tracked us down.

We liked Corfu, especially the parts of the island where there were no tourists, and we viewed a few houses. But everything seemed to be rather overpriced and there appeared to be too many Brits already in residence. Instead we settled for Crete because it was a bigger island, potent with the myth of Theseus and the Minotaur and stuffed with relics of ancient civilizations. And, of course, I had that memory from my teens of one intoxicating evening in Heraklion. Moonlight on the water, stuffed vine leaves, retsina, the faint sound of bouzouki music from a nearby taverna and nearly my first kiss. Quite enough to build a new future on.

Then my mother had her stroke. It was coming up for her seventieth birthday. She had arranged for the local hunt to meet at her farm. She had hunted since she was four-years-old. I have a picture of her somewhere sitting on a tiny pony with her father on a huge hunter towering above her. Everyone turned up. All her friends from the hunt. The hunt followers. Lots of other people. Someone had made her a cake. I think she was quite overwhelmed.

Adam and his cousin spent all day out on the farm watching the horses and putting themselves in considerable danger. At one point they told me they were hiding under a hedge when the hunt were jumping it. They could very easily have been killed. My comfort is that the last real memory of their grandmother is of her fearlessly galloping off into the distance. That night she was felled.

She had always had a terror of hospitals so we didn't immediately send her in for observation which was probably a huge mistake. I think the doctor thought she might die, so he didn't interfere. She went to a nursing home for a while but she hated that so we had some private nursing at home. After a while my brother and his wife decided they could cope as she was living in a converted barn on the farm and would be near enough for them to look after her.

It was a huge stroke which left her half-paralysed and unable to speak in most circumstances. But she could come out with some complete and splendid pleasantries. I determined to try and get her speaking again. I made an appointment with the speech therapist at the local hospital. It was like taking a reluctant child to school. I more or less dragged her through the corridors to the consulting room where we found a very sweet young woman surrounded with what looked like primary school teaching materials. I could see my mother taking this in.

The therapist explained that this would only work if my mother was willing to make an effort. I said, 'Shall we just try and see what happens?'

The therapist looks at my mother and says, 'Now, Mrs Barlow would you repeat after me: *my house is by the post office?*'

Mother looks at her blankly.

'My house is by the post office,' the therapist says again.

At which point my mother sits up, looks her straight in the eye and says, 'How nice for you.'

I took her home.

I think now, if I'd persisted, or got some more expert help, she might have regained her speech, but I was still in a strange, detached state and not much good for anything that involved concentration. In fact, of course, I didn't really want to believe the mother I'd known was gone.

On one occasion, I heard the hunt close to the farm and got her up on her horse to see whether this would reawaken the person she once was. Luckily we never got close, as I think the horse would have taken off and she might never have come back. Perhaps, on the other hand, that would have been how she would have liked to have gone?

As it was she lived for nine more years, first in the barn, then in part of my brother's house when they moved again. Here she behaved rather like a naughty child wandering round the garden and pulling up priceless plants. She had always liked gardening and shadows of other rituals remained. She would tap the table every evening at six o'clock and inform everyone it was 'drink time'.

I suppose this could have stopped Persey and I going to Greece, but we were both in the process of selling our houses and I felt I needed to get away – to escape my isolation and/or find a place where William could be with me. I was ever hopeful and things seemed to be going my way. He was back in Australia again. The marriage seemed to be failing and he had gone to try and build himself a new life.

I persuaded Desmond to phone William's wife to find an address for him. I wrote to him telling him what was going on and suggesting he came to Greece with us. His response was a letter asking for a loan so that he could come back. The last time I'd seen him we'd had an argument in the street and I had no idea how he was going react. At the time there were fires raging in Australia.

*Dear Peps,*

*So good to hear from you. I had thought that was it, our last goodbye, our final curtain call, our last explosion. We seem to have an unerring skill in bringing our emotions up to the boil at what always seems to be the wrong time. Perhaps it's the right time.*

*I have a studio on top of an antique shop and have hung up my shingle along with some tired old paintings of mine and await recognition and money from non-existent buyers. Am gasping for breath in the infernal hell of this climate. I have lost a friend in the fires and it's been incredible to re-experience the raw savagery of this country. What a marvellous romantic fabulous idea, to go to a Greek Island!! But wait – isn't Corfu full of tourists?? Yes it is. Try some other place. Maybe Ios??*

*If you could lend me some money to get back to England, please – £1000 – £3000 would do. Will pay you back. If not, that's Okay. I will swim. It may take longer that's all. I have been sick with sinus trouble. Lost a lot of weight. Many X-rays and antibiotics, lots*

*of doctor's fees and I am broke – not in spirit – not
yet. Not ever.*

*I have done this series of paintings called
'Cosmic Books'. Seven books of forty pages.
Incredible explosions of colour – mind blowing – I
did them in a creative burst of energy, between 2-4 in
the morning when it cooled down. I feel so good about
these 'Cosmic Books'. My next series are 'Cosmic
Dancers on a Cloud of Unknowing'. I hope to show
these as 'Pages from my Cosmic Books' in London in
May. I hope you will see them and like them. They are
really an extension of my 'Medieval Images' without
figures. Works on paper, non-figurative.*

*What have we got you and I – can you define our
relationship into terms – maybe one world would
suffice?*

*Love William*

The sale of my house came through. I sent William
some money and rented a farmhouse where I waited for him
to join us. He came back, borrowed a cottage from a friend
and I expected him daily. On the day he actually arrived I
had taken my mother to visit an aunt. When I came back –
after three years remember – I found a note pinned to the
door. YOU'RE NEVER HERE WHEN I NEED YOU.
ODYSSEUS. You had to give him marks for timing!

He came and lived in the farmhouse with me for three
days and then went back to his cottage. I was too intense.
He was riding a storm of his own. We didn't appear to be
able to live under the same roof. He did however, in a
rather half-hearted way, join in a plan for all four of us to
set up a business in Crete together. William would run art
courses. Persey and I were going to create courses in self-
awareness. (Yes, don't laugh.) Not sure what Desmond

was planning on but he was probably going to be good at lifting heavy objects and keeping Persey happy. All seemed set.

Persey and I were going to set out first with the children. We decided we would go by boat. We both wanted to take our cars and I suppose we both felt a kind of misplaced nostalgia for our parents' voyages and the fun we thought they'd had on their journeys back and forth around the Empire. We also had a view that if we just got on a plane and arrived the same day we would not have any sense of the significance of the journey we were making.

I rang the Port of London Authority and asked if passage on a cargo ship was still a possibility? They said, yes, but we would have to wait for a suitable conveyance. They would get back to me. In the interim I moved back into my mother's house to await confirmation of our passage.

At this time William's wife had gone to Australia to officiate at the marriage of her younger sister. William had been left to look after the children and I saw quite a lot of him. He was still talking about coming to Greece and we seemed to be getting on alright so I was hopeful. We heard from the Port of London. A ship would be sailing from Bristol in October. They were willing to take us. William said he would drive down to join us when the mood took him. All seemed set.

There was one rather odd moment. We were lying on a grassy bank in a wood somewhere. Very Shakespearean. He had his eyes shut. I was stroking his hair. He had a rather strange shaped head. His forehead sloped back quite dramatically. I remember thinking, *I would recognise you on a battlefield. I could find you even if you were dead.*

Then his wife came home and he set out to go to the studio in France where he usually spent his summers.

*The hills around Quetta are beautiful and I would have ridden or walked in them, as you must have done, had it not been for the rain which kept me in the town – a lot of the time being spent in the chai houses there for that reason. However, I can't imagine how all you British got on there. I mean, the town itself, of which I was so fond, is so seedy – all makeshift shacks for shops and chai stalls, and there was only one 'decent' restaurant in the whole town that I could find. I took a Nigerian Muslim to dinner there after taking his very beautiful hand-embroidered shawl off him. He really liked it, poor man, but it looks much better on me and have been looking for such a shawl for ages. He said it had sentimental attachments for him so I said it was time they came to an end!*

# STRENGTH

*I made beautiful cloth. I make beautiful cloth. My weaving
was like a spell calling you home. Colours and patterns,
things you might remember. Silver and green for the olive
leaf. Blue and gold for the sea. I thought with every cloth I
wove, with every skein I laid out in the sun to dry, you would
come back to me.*

*TROJAN WHORES*

I was staying in my mother's cottage. The phone went. It
was about eleven in the morning. I answered it. It was
William's wife. She asked if I had anyone with me? I said
there were people around.

'It's William. He's had a car crash in France.'

I stood with the phone in my hand and I knew.

'Is he dead?' I ask.

'Yes. His car came off the road. He died instantly.'

I felt strangely calm. I think she expected me to break
down. It was difficult in those days for me to tell which
parts of my journey were real or imaginary. This is an event
of epic importance. Part of me is already fitting it into the
mythology that was our journey. Another part of me is
screaming.

'Where is he?'

'In Chateauroux. They took him to the hospital. I'll
collect him on the way.'

'Way to where?'

'I think he'd want to be buried in Conques. He loved it
there.'

'Well, yes, I suppose so. Thank you for letting me
know.'

'Will you be all right?'

'I'll live,' I say, 'thank you.'

My first instinct is to go and find Persey. Drive up the hill where I had walked for so long. Where William had lived for a few months in the house down the road. Where he had sometimes walked with me. I want to touch the landscape we had shared.

Persey is hanging up the washing. There is a wind. The sheets are blowing out like sails. I can see her feet below the sheets. Her hands pegging the cloth as she moves along the line. My mind goes to winding sheets and the need to know that it is true. To make it real.

'William's dead,' I say, to a sheet with hands.

The hands stop. The familiar face appears around the cloth. 'What?'

'He died in France. On the way to the studio. He's in some mortuary somewhere.'

'Are you sure?'

'His wife rang.'

The rest of her appears round the sheet. 'Oh my god. What do you want to do?'

'I want to go. I must go.' I say. 'I'm not sure *he* knows he's dead.'

'Then I'll go with you,' she says.

And that was that. We picked up our two youngest sons, recruited Desmond as the driver and booked the ferry to France. Adam was with his father in Ireland.

'This is just another place on the journey. I'll be alright, I'm going to survive this.' I kept saying to myself.

I was alright until the ferry set out to sea. Something about leaving the shore, about being on the water. I started crying and couldn't stop. I felt as though I was pouring my sorrow into the universe. That I would be empty by the time we reached the other side.

Persey amused the kids. Desmond filled me full of brandy. And somehow I survived. We drove out of the port and I was sane again. Sane being a relative term, of course. Desmond and Persey sat in the front of the car having an ongoing argument about what kind of house they might like to live in together. I was in the back with the boys. We drove for hours, heading for Chateauroux and the mortuary.

At one point I am wondering how I am going to live with this when William is suddenly inhabiting my body. I look down and there are his hands. Here he is and this is an approximation of what we said to each other. Me first, since I was the only one left.

'Hello, what's a nice guy like you doing in a place like this?'

*'I don't know. Am I dead?'*

'So they tell me.'

*'So we've only got one body between us then?'*

'Seems like it.'

*'You'd better bunk up then.'*

'*Now* he wants to be with me!' I say to the imaginary him.

*'You only ever wanted me for my body,'* he says.

I laugh. See Desmond check me out in the mirror. We drive on.

We arrived in Chateauroux late in the evening and stopped at a police station to get directions. They told us where to find the hospital but said the mortuary would be closed until morning. So we found an auberge. Went for supper – kept an extra place for William – and enjoyed a beautiful meal, the kind that only the French can provide.

Lying in bed with his son asleep beside me. An open window. The warmth of a summer's night. And then thunder. Lightning. Pouring rain. The child wakes. I tell him not to worry, that his father is riding around on a motorbike in the sky, enjoying himself. That his father is now in charge of the weather.

Next morning we went to the mortuary. Parked outside.

Desmond said he would come in with me. We left Persey playing on the grass with the boys.

Inside I explained in my schoolgirl French, that I had come to see William. The mortician, a rather worried-looking man in a white coat, said to wait. He would get the body ready. Desmond asked if I wanted him to come in with me? I said no, I wanted to see him on my own.

The mortician returned. I understood him to say that William's face was marked. He'd washed the blood off, but did I want him to cover his face? I said, 'No.'

I began to imagine an unholy mess and thought William, who was always very neat and tidy and not a little vain about his looks, would not have liked to be seen to his disadvantage. The mortician showed me into a little room like a chapel. There was a stained glass window. A body on a bier.

I suppose I expected him to be naked. But there he was, still dressed in his pink shirt and slacks. His shoes laid neatly beside his feet. I was glad of the familiarity of his clothes. He had been in the freezer for several days and didn't look quite like himself. More like a waxwork. His face was only a bit off-centre. He'd obviously sustained a heavy blow to the head. But no blood. His dark hair combed. His hands. I recognised his hands.

I stood there filled with grief and rage. What was I going to do? I'd have hit him if he'd been alive.

I'd brought a piece of Shakespeare to read to him. The dirge for Fidele from *Cymbeline*. I take it out. I read.

*Fear no more the heat o' the sun,*
*Nor the furious winter's rages;*
*Thou thy worldly task hast done,*
*Home art gone, and ta'en thy wages:*
*Golden lads and girls all must,*
*As chimney-sweepers, come to dust.*

*Fear no more the frown o' the great,*
*Thou art past the tyrant's stroke:*
*Care no more to clothe and eat;*
*To thee the reed is as the oak:*
*The sceptre, learning, physic, must*
*All follow this, and come to dust.*

*Fear no more the lightning-flash,*
*Nor the all-dreaded thunder-stone;*
*Fear not slander, censure rash;*
*Thou hast finish'd joy and moan;*
*All lovers young, all lovers must*
*Consign to thee, and come to dust.*

*No exorciser harm thee!*
*Nor no witchcraft charm thee!*
*Nothing ill come near thee!*
*Quiet consummation have;*
*And renowned be thy grave!*

As I was speaking I felt William standing somewhere watching me. Imagined him saying, 'Oh, this is good, women coming to weep over me.' Although I'm not sure I wept. Not then. It all seemed much the same as usual. Me telling him I loved him. Him not saying much.

Then Desmond put his head round the door. The mortician was on the phone to his supervisor and wanted to give me the body. I tucked the piece of paper into William's shirt pocket and followed Desmond into the mortician's office. He was still on the phone looking worried. He handed it to me so I could speak to the supervisor. I managed to say, in my very imperfect French, that I was not his wife, I was his friend. His wife would be coming on Sunday. Why Sunday? I could only

71

remember the word for Sunday. I had no idea when she would come.

I gave the phone back to the mortician. He spoke to his supervisor again. Put the phone down and beamed. 'Ah,' he said in French, 'you are not his wife. You are his friend.' This was love. He liked that. I thought about what the reaction would have been in England at the time. I imagined the atmosphere turning to ice and being, not very politely, shown the door.

We went out to join Persey playing with the boys in the sun. Told her we could have brought William with us.

'Not in my car,' she said. 'He was enough trouble while he was alive. Don't want him stinking us out now.'

What to do next? I wanted to go on to Conques, to the studio. I wanted to complete the journey he had started. If he was riding with us in a non-corporeal form that was important.

Later, much later, I wrote a play based on the mortuary moment but this time I used a passage from Antony and Cleopatra. He was, after all my Antony. My Odysseus. My Theseus. One of any number of heroes my mother had infected me with. If this was a story I was going to make into a good one.

---

*Don't think I told you that I got on to the wrong train at Quetta, saw someone I knew so got off and took them for tea and when I got back to the platform the train had departed with ALL my precious belongings. By the time I had made the discovery my 'proper' train was almost due to depart. Went to the Station Master who phoned the next station and told them to take my luggage off the train, where I collected it all an hour later.*

---

# THE HERMIT

*And then I woke one morning in my empty bed and knew
that I was dying. That my whole life was being eaten away
by the waiting. No one knew me. No one, not even my son
would miss me. He had already left to look for you. If I died
that day it would be a dark, lonely death with people
whispering in the shadows. No one to hold me. No one to
miss me. No one there. If you ever did come home you
probably wouldn't even miss me. They could dress any
woman in my clothes and tell you she was your wife.
Probably better if they did. Twenty years and how many
women later? Why would you want an old wife who had
dried up waiting for you? Why would I want a dried-up old
husband, drained of life by the war? Suddenly I wanted to
know what it was like to set sail and not know when or if I
was ever coming home? Suddenly I wanted to know what it
was like to meet death on the battlefield.*

*TROJAN WHORES*

Conques is a medieval village in the mountains, a place of
pilgrimage. The saint, St. Foy, was a simple girl who spoke
out against the church for investing in so much wealth and
power. The Abbey in Conques was founded in 866 AD and
her relics were stolen from somewhere else, so that it would
have a decent shrine to attract pilgrims on their way to
Compostela. A role it still plays today.

Turning the corner and catching sight of the village
perched on the hillside must be heart-stopping moment at
any time, but when you are carrying the ghost of a dead
lover to his final resting place it has celestial impact.

William had spent his last summer there, on his own,
drawing endless pictures of the Cathars being slaughtered.
Where that came from I didn't know? Perhaps it was how

73

he felt? Perhaps it was a memory of something, a past life? Perhaps it had soaked into the stones? All I knew was that I had seen him slaughtered and I needed to know the place where he would come to rest.

I think I expected to see these images in the gallery on which he had turned the key the previous summer. But when we found the keys to his house and went in the walls were hung with angels. Angels in every form. Blue and gold and green. A keyhole in the shape of an angel. A white dove poised over a font against a background of vivid pink. His Catholic upbringing coming back into focus.

We went into the church. I lit candles. I sat in the side chapel dedicated to Saint Foy and remembered him saying he had heard her say. 'You are my little angel.'

I sat with her now and heard nothing. But it was strangely comforting to know this was where he had been.

That night Persey and Desmond took the boys and stayed in a hotel at the bottom of the hill. I slept alone in the bed he must have been the last to leave. The only evidence of his presence, a used toothbrush in a glass and a pair of shorts in a cupboard. It was one of the most peaceful nights I've ever had. In my strangely-ordered mind I felt I had him to myself at last.

I woke to sounds in the square below. Looking out of the window I examined the image of heaven and hell carved over the doorway to the church. Hoped that William's Catholicism wouldn't condemn him to any such experience.

I dressed and went back down to the chapel. Lit another candle and said a quiet prayer for his safe journey in whichever place he found himself. Asked Saint Foy to look after him.

Later I was to experience the past life which seemed to connect us to this place. In that he was my son and the saint indeed called him her 'little angel'.

Going back out into the square bright with sunlight, I hear my name being called from the direction of the house. *My god*, I think, *he's getting good at this.* I look up to see Persey standing in the upstairs window. She is short and dark as he had been. She'd do as a channel.

We went back down the hill to find Desmond and the children playing by the river and they took me home. Back through summer storms and lightning. That summer was full of storms.

On the day of his funeral I went up to our place on the hill and decided to walk the circuit as I had done during all those years of waiting. I set out in bright sunlight, turned right at the church and walked down towards the valley. As I reached the bottom of the hill the heavens opened. Thunder. Lightning. Hailstones the size of marbles. All very dramatic. I took shelter for a while in a wood by the road.

As I stood under a tree watching the deluge, there was a crack overhead and I realised that a bolt of lightning had hit the telegraph pole just a few feet away from me.

'OK,' I say. 'I'll come if you want me to.'

But as ever he wandered off and when the thunder sounded again the storm had moved down the valley.

When I arrived back at the church there were piles of hailstones banked against the walls and the sun was out again. The elements were certainly doing their dramatic bit.

I had timed my arrival at the church for the start of his funeral in France. I learned later that he kept everyone in Conques waiting. The hearse got stuck behind a farm vehicle coming up the mountain road and there were people standing around in the square for more than an hour. Late for his own funeral. Right on time for delivering me a parting lightning strike.

What I had left of him is his son. Bun used to say to me when I was upset and he was young, 'He left you me as a present, Mum.' I couldn't argue with that. I also have some of his pictures. A sketch of my two cats beside the Rayburn in the cottage. A small watercolour of strange, mythical figures which he painted in Greece and gave me for my birthday. A medieval figure in a red costume, *The Falconer*, a picture I bought when he was alive and I was still hoping he'd become more than just a mythical figure in my landscape. And, of course, I have one of his angels. My blue angel. It sits beside my bed and I talk to it as I've always talked to him.

At some point Persey read an article in *Cosmopolitan* which said, 'All ex-lovers should either go to Australia or die.' I had to give him credit, he did both.

---

*The journey from Quetta to Zaidan was a mixed up affair. They put all the foreigners, including me, in one carriage. As usual got dragged off for chai and meals in different carriages which was all very jolly until the night when I had a dreadful time for a couple of hours with a carriage full of smugglers cum bandits who I'm sure would have raped me had I lost my cool. However, after a couple of hours having a bad time with that lot, a policeman rescued me and took me to the police carriage where was given a really cosy and comfortable bed roll (without bugs) and slept a peaceful and undisturbed night.*

---

# THE WHEEL OF FORTUNE

*I must have fallen asleep. I woke to the sun and the boat bumping in the surf. I was near land. I fell from the boat into the water. Fought my way through the waves. And now I'm here. But where am I? Where is this place?*

*TROJAN WHORES*

We might at this point have decided not to go to Greece. But to me it felt as though we had already set out on the journey. William was just the first casualty, the one who fell overboard. Shortly after that the dog died and Desmond was told he wasn't coming with us. So that just left Persey, me and the four boys. Her daughter was going to stay with her father.

We had booked passage on a car transporter which was leaving from Bristol.

We drove our cars to Bristol, only to be told that sailing was delayed as the cargo was not complete. While we waited we stayed in one room in a hotel with two of the boys sleeping on the luggage rack.

Then the call came and we set out to find the ship. I drove down to the dock with my boys in the back of the car. In the distance I noticed a huge rusting hulk and remarked to the children, 'No one in their right mind would go to sea in that.'

Needless to say, when we got closer and I could read the name on the peeling prow, I realized that this was the boat we were booked to sail in.

The captain and crew were Italian and it wasn't at all clear they had been informed about our arrival, but they rose to the occasion with customary charm. At first we were shown to the crews' quarters. Bleak, empty cabins below the waterline with iron bunks. We couldn't really complain but it was not very cheerful and there must have been some kind of consultation upstairs because we were soon found rooms in the officers' quarters with proper bunk beds and showers in the corner of the cabins. Still not very salubrious, but at least we could see daylight.

We were told to leave our car keys with the first mate and our luggage was brought to our cabins. We woke at sea and found the first mate looking rather sheepish. They had been at the point of casting off when he put his hand in his pocket, felt the keys, and remembered what they were for.

We soon settled into the routine. Breakfast was early, lunch at eleven and a much lighter evening meal around six. None of us were really hungry enough for the early lunch but as we discovered the cook had killed his wife, not necessarily because she didn't eat all her food, everyone, even the children, ate what they were given. It was lovely food, so it was no great hardship.

The days were filled with keeping the children amused. Everyone joined in. It was quite usual to find the Chief Engineer wandering about with a child on his arm or the cook playing cards with the older boys. This was especially interesting to Persey and I as they used a Tarot pack to play Tarocchi, a card game rather like Bridge. Here were the images we had consulted as we mapped our journey through life being used to amuse our children.

First port of call was Rotterdam where we went to the Zoo. Then out across the Bay of Biscay. I had been dreading this. Endless tales of bad weather and one story of a car transporter that had snapped in half. We hadn't been given any safety instructions and I had the feeling it would be a very *ad hoc* affair if the ship sank. Can't even remember if there was a lifeboat.

In the event the Bay of Biscay was like a millpond and I spent one blissful evening sitting on a corner of the deck with stars above and the lights of passing ships reflected in the water. At some point I heard a cough and saw the dark shape of the Chief Engineer lit by a cigarette not far away from me. The Captain had taken a shine to Persey and she had taken up residence in his cabin, claiming it was the only way of getting a decent bath. They were now busy trying to get me together with the Chief Engineer who was a nice enough looking chap but, since we had only a few words in common, and I was still in a state of shock, nothing was going to happen there. Besides someone had to keep an eye on the children.

Next port of call was Malta. We had been going rather slowly, I thought. The Captain kept telling us he was avoiding bad weather ahead. I suspected he was enjoying Persey's company far too much and was in no great hurry to arrive. But when we got to Malta there were signs of storm-force winds, bits of trees all over the roads, and I realized he'd been telling the truth.

We were given a day to explore and arrived in the Cathedral in Valletta to be confronted by still more images straight from the Tarot. Everywhere, on the graves of the Knights of Malta, were the archetypal images of *Death* reaping his harvest, *The Tower* broken by a feather. Given my current state of mind this was an extraordinary experience, the message being that this reality, the one we were travelling through, was only one of many. Death just a doorway. Of course, I took it personally, as a sign that William was not very far away.

Then on to Piraeus where the ship was going to leave us. We arrived in the port at dawn. I stood on the deck watching the shipping and trying to remember that in Greece it is rude to show the palm of your hand when you wave.

As soon as we had docked there was a problem.

Apparently our cars weren't on the manifest and were to be impounded in the dock until we got the right papers. We were ferried into Piraeus in a rowing boat, taken to a small hotel and then set out to find the shipping company to try to sort things out. At first they didn't want to know but we behaved like travellers of old and rang the British Consul who was not very sympathetic either and assured us we had a problem. He did, however, agree to have a conversation with the shipping company and we were eventually allotted a young man with a squeaky voice who spoke good English. He took us back to the port where we became involved in a pantomime of labyrinthine proportions.

First of all, we were informed, we needed a 'lawyer' to lead us through. He was going to cost money and we had no way of knowing if the man we chose was going to deliver the goods. But squeaky man said he was alright and we really had no choice.

At this point we all piled into the lawyer's car and were taken to various offices. First complication was that I didn't have the logbook for my car, only a note of sale, as the logbook had gone to be registered in my name and hadn't been returned in time. Everyone was shouting in Greek. I shouted in English, assuring the man that I wouldn't have this bit of paper if I didn't own the car. After some time the official we had all been shouting at said, in immaculate English, 'Madam, there is no need to shout.' He stamped the relevant piece of paper as though it was nothing at all.

But this was not enough. We needed more papers and more stamps and if we didn't get them all before midday when everyone clocked off we would have to wait till the next day and start all over again. More rushing around, more officials, more shouting. Eventually the lawyer grabbed a stamp and franked all the papers himself. It didn't seem to matter which stamp it was. There were dozens of them.

Fifteen minutes to go and we were on the way to our cars when the lawyer informs us we have to pay storage fees. I protest. I never asked them to store my car and the figure he mentions is more than we have paid for all the proceedings so far. He screeches the car to a halt, leans over the seat, fixes me with a steely gaze and says, 'You want your cars, you don't want your cars?' We agree to pay.

We leave the dock with two pieces of paper duly stamped and proceed to book the ferry to Crete. We are on the last stage of our journey. By this time Persey and I are not really speaking to each other, I can't remember why, and I note she slips off to make a phone call. We arrive in Iraklion and present our papers. They are very good papers but we are told they will have to have them validated within the month. More of that later.

First, we thought, maybe the west of the island and the old port of Hania would be a good destination and duly found a place to stay near the beach. Then food and shopping. I had been working away at my Linguaphone Greek and knew a few phrases. Trouble was that lots of words in Greek sounded much the same to me and I only had a very sketchy idea of the syntax. I managed to ask for bread but didn't seem to be having much luck with eggs. Eventually I resorted to clucking and pretending to lay them, much to the amusement of the shopkeeper who marched round the shop crowing like a cockerel and returned with the required items. The word for 'slowly' (*arga*) and the word for 'egg' (*avga*) being quite similar, I decided I had probably been asking for six 'slowlies'.

Next we went looking for houses to rent. We were shown some very nice houses but they all seemed to be perched around a bay that was home to the military and we were warned not to go down to the beach or take photographs on pain of death. We began to think of other places that might be more suitable.

Meanwhile the phone call Persey had made in Piraeus manifested Desmond, with whom she proceeded to have rather frightening arguments, one of which involved him throwing her car keys into an orange grove and a man chasing us out with a gun when we went to look for them. I think Desmond wanted her to go back to England with him and was none too pleased to find he was being used to cheer her up in Greece. Anyway he stayed, and we set off for the other end of the island.

We arrived in Agios Nikolaos late one evening and found a small hotel near the bus station. Here I decided to practice a few more words of Greek. I approached the woman at the desk and thought I told her we were three adults and four children and we wanted rooms for the night. She looked a bit confused so I repeated my statement, more slowly and in a louder voice. Really, could she not understand her own language? She didn't look any more enlightened but obviously decided to take matters into her own hands. She took some keys and led us to a couple of perfectly adequate rooms, waved her hands about a bit and left us to settle in.

It was only weeks later when we had found the villas we were to live in that I tried to work out what she might have thought I said. The closest we came was that I had pronounced the following: 'We are three sisters (one of them being Desmond) and four children and we are invisible on Thursdays.'

I did note that when I met her in town on any subsequent Thursday she pretended not to see me. Well, actually she pretended not to see me any day of the week, Thursdays included.

*It's no good telling you my plans for sure as I often change them, e.g. decided to go direct to from Zaidan at one point but had a whole $100 to my name when getting into Iran (out of $300 I left Mashad to go to Kashmir with) so it seemed crazy not to do some more travelling whilst in this part of the country, which I haven't seen before. When in such towns as this I praise Allah that I always rushed back to you before rather than doing any real travelling. I mean, Kerman is so wild that even I return to my hotel by 7.00 pm or so (instead of the normal midnight) and they would not take kindly to a half-mental Christian tourist as opposed to a fully-fledged Moslem traveller!!!*

# JUSTICE

*When he loved me I was the most wonderful creature in the world. And everything about us was clear and bright and bathed in light. When he didn't he was gone into a great dark underground cavern and I was the toothless hag holding him away from everything he held most dear.*

*DEAD END*

Agios Nikolaos is a town that explodes during the tourist season. In winter it goes quiet. Most of the tavernas and cafés had closed down and it was hard to get served in the ones which were open as the owner was nearly always engaged in a game of backgammon and didn't want to be disturbed.

We set out to find somewhere to live. A friend had given us the name of a taverna – the 'Taverna Olga' – on the coast road. We went in the general direction of. No one seemed to know where the place was, but in travelling up into the hills behind the town we saw 'Villa Olga' painted on a rough sign on the side of the road. This was the name we wanted but there was no taverna in sight. But perhaps it was a clue? There was a telephone number. I rang it. I spoke some words in what might have been Greek and was given to understand that the son would be home later and he spoke English. It turned out that the notice referred to two holiday villas and we could rent them for the year.

Persey took the larger villa with the television and a bath. I got the smaller villa above with a small balcony looking out over the mountains and the sea and enough room for the three of us.

There were also cats. Our landlord owned a bus and stopped by each day to feed the cats and see we were all right. Shortly after our arrival there was a litter of kittens

84

and both my children took one on. Bun's kitten was a tom and he called it Tom so there was no confusion and he carried it everywhere. By the end of the year they were inseparable. When I drove the car into the parking bay beneath the villa Tom cat would arrive and be carried up to the villa by his small owner even when he was huge and his feet touched the ground. The other kitten was called Fluff and didn't have quite such a central role in Adam's life. Adam was nine and his joy was in going off on adventures with Persey's children and, later, when they left, finding new friends each fortnight and initiating them into the mysteries of his island home.

But first there was the matter of Persey's car. Having survived the experience in Piraeus we had been given to understand we had to register the cars again when we reached Crete. But Persey had lost the magic piece of stamped paper and all sorts of complications ensued. Eventually we ended up at the Customs House in Agios Nikolaos with the customs official telling her she would have to go back to England and start again.

'Right,' says Persey, looking out at the bright green Alfa Romeo that was the car in question. 'If you won't let me keep my car I shall go out now and push it into the dock and that will give you another kind of problem.' Note again that in Greece at the time cars were more expensive than houses.

The customs official looked at the assembled men. There was always an assembly of men if there was a problem to be solved. Looked at us. Looked at the car. And then picked up the stamp. Persey got to keep her car.

The next thing was to get the children into school. More officials. More half-understood conversations before the two older boys were duly enrolled. After a few days being taken in by car they learnt to take the bus which was often driven by our landlord. They met us after school in a café in town for lunch and then we all went to the beach for the afternoon. Later Persey's daughter joined us and she also went to school, although as far as we could tell none of them learnt any Greek and nobody seemed to take much notice of them.

At least that's what I was given to understand. According to Persey the boys would go in through the school gates, go to class for assembly and then abscond and explore the town. Once the summer arrived they sampled all the swimming pools in the big hotels and arrived at the café just in time to meet us for lunch. Persey didn't tell me because she thought I would have been cross with Adam and they certainly didn't seem to come to any harm.

Adam now has a PhD in Environmental Science and has worked to conserve tigers in the wild. If anything I think the year in Crete gave him a sense in which his life was his own and he could be Luke Skywalker if he wanted. All the children at the time were into *Star Wars* and we had come out armed with boxes full of Star Wars figures. Indeed I spent my fortieth birthday in an outdoor cinema watching *The Return of the Jedi*, subtitled in Greek. Bun was really too young to notice. They told him he was an Ewok and bundled him along with them.

We were all fired up with stories. Greek myths. *Star Wars*. Some strange heroic figures we bought in a shop in town for Christmas. A chess set peopled with figures from the story of Theseus and the Minotaur. All of us were on our own mythical journey.

But back to reality. The villas were built on the outskirts of a village. We just had to walk up the hill, behind a few houses where the women lit their fires each night to cook supper, and there we were. There was a Café Neon where all the men assembled, a couple of what looked like ponds and olive groves which ran down the valley and up into the hills beyond. Persey and I made the fatal mistake of thinking we could join the men in the café, the scene of all sorts of strange dramas and misunderstandings as time went on with the women assembled in the doorway to watch.

One of the first problems was the business of finding wood. There was no central heating and the nights were getting colder. We both had open fireplaces but no idea how to fuel them. Persey decided we needed a chainsaw. We got one. This made us instantly popular with villagers who wanted to trim their olive trees. So one afternoon we were whisked away by a neighbour to the olive grove where his family had ten trees. He did a lot of pruning and there was a moment when we thought he would like us to cut the whole tree down for him. Thank goodness we couldn't remember where it was. Olive trees take years to grow and are handed down through the generations. Not being able to understand the language had its drawbacks. Actually I could say one very complex sentence that I had learnt from my Linguaphone kit, namely '*My central heating pipes are situated beneath the window.*' Singularly useless in the circumstances.

So, no central heating pipes but a need for wood. We set out into the countryside in our cars. First we found what looked like an abandoned telegraph pole. It had clearly been replaced so we cut it up and took it home. Just as we arrived, the landlord appeared and was horrified. There was a label on the poll which indicated government property and he clearly thought we were all going to be arrested. So, no more telegraph polls. Then we took to spotting branches of oak trees lying on the ground. Those must surely be fair game. So into the fields we went and took what we could cut up.

On one of these forays a man appeared with a shotgun and threatened us with death. I think he thought we were cutting down his olive trees. By that time I understood the word for kill and leaned back on the bonnet of my car and said – in perfect Greek – 'And then what will you do?' Then his daughter arrived and got a fix on what was happening and we were all invited back to their house for raki and cakes. We later realized that the felled branches had been left to season and were meant for collection later. Wood was in very short supply and we were stealing it. We were lucky we weren't killed.

The next drama was the *sterna*. A sterna is a tank for storing water. There was a meeting in the Café Neon to which we were summoned. People in the village had seen our children playing by the sterna and they were worried they would fall in. Persey decided they were trying to tell us how to bring our children up and took umbrage. A minor shouting match ensued and we retreated more than a little confused. I walked round the village for days looking for this dangerous water tank and only later, when it was the summer and the water retreated, realized that the two ponds we let the children paddle in were actually yards deep and they could easily have drowned. The villagers were just trying to look after them and us.

We made various friends. One man was very keen to feed us traditional Greek food. He arrived in the villa duly equipped and did a lot of pot banging. Eventually we all assembled at the table and he took the lid of the saucepan to reveal a whole sheep's head, eyes and all, looking up at us. You have never seen children leave a table so quickly. He told us the brain was very good for us, but they were not to be persuaded.

On another occasion, we were walking in the hills and came across a family having a picnic. Of course we were asked to join them and people started spooning food into our mouths. Persey tasted hers with good grace and, fairly sure that no one would understand her, smiled sweetly and said, 'Hm, disgusting.' And was promptly fed some more. We had this vision afterwards of these kind people repeating her phrase at all sorts of family celebrations. Or not as the case may be.

It was interesting being foreigners in a place where foreigners were only ever tourists. In the winter we became honorary Greeks. We had learned enough of the language to shop and pass pleasantries so when the real tourists arrived we were already one of the locals.

Another advantage of the winter is that you can roam the big tourist sites without fear of interruption. In our first week we went to Knossos to see the site of the Labyrinth and the bullring. We had all read *The King Must Die* and *The Bull from the Sea* by Mary Renault and could imagine the bull dancers and the young men sent for sacrifice.

Meanwhile I felt as though I had died and arrived in the Elysian Fields with no map home. William's wraith still haunted me and as usual I was more comfortable travelling the underworld than in dealing with life as it was. My children say that they had a wonderful time in Greece except that every afternoon their mother went to bed and cried. But I hadn't entirely given up. I expected this mythical landscape to deliver me the living as well as the dead.

---

*Did I tell you I am considered to be a Holy traveller by many people here? For example, I was carried out of the mosque in Mashad one time after prayers and two or three thousand people followed me into the enormous courtyard where I sang the Beatles song 'All You Need Is Love' before departing. Must say, that was the most fulfilling theatrical moment of my life – I mean, a one woman show to such a huge audience – who could resist?!*

---

# THE HANGED MAN

*Are you sure you're not shamming it? It's just the sort of
thing you'd do. So I'd come and play the death scene. Tell
you how wonderful you are and how I can't live without
you. You'd love that, wouldn't you?'*

*DEAD END*

When we first arrived at the village there was a notice on
the road which read both in Greek and English: *SITE OF
APHRODITE*. At first we were too busy to bother about it
but as the days drew on and the winter set in we would
occasionally enquire, 'Where is the site of Aphrodite?' in
Greek and English as we had both mastered 'where is' by
then.

This resulted in various responses. First and foremost
was the great Greek shrug which could mean, who cares,
who knows, why should I tell you, and only a fool or a
foreigner would ask such a silly question? And then of
course the men would wink and say they'd show us
Aphrodite any time we wanted. But no one volunteered to
take us to the site. We couldn't see anything that looked out
of the ordinary and began to wonder if it actually existed.

Both Persey and I were looking for love in our own
ways. I had been taken with the owner of a little bar by the
beach called Manolis, largely because he looked a bit like
William. Not tall, but dark, warm, and entirely enchanted
by women. Real *Shirley Valentine* stuff. We met while we
were looking for somewhere to live and since he didn't
seem to mind us taking the children into the bar, we all went
there most evenings. After some standard flattery, the odd
kiss and much singing of songs on the bouzouki he asked if
he could come up and find me at the villa. I was completely
at sea and he seemed to be a nice man so I gave him

instructions and, sure enough, at about one o'clock in the morning he appeared.

This was going to be our first night of passion and I had decided to look forward to it. Only hitch was it was election night and he was not going to miss a moment of it. So while he was making perfunctory love to me, we had the radio blasting away in Greek at the bedside accompanied by occasional passionate exclamations from him entirely related to the election results. By the end of the evening I knew my place.

Of course he was used to women coming and going with fortnightly regularity but I stayed and this rather spoilt his pitch. To begin with he tried to palm me off with any stray man in the bar but I did have my standards. One night I was reading palms in a desultory manner, as you do when wintering on a Greek island, and Manolis appeared with an unprepossessing middle-aged man and sat him down beside me. He informed me the man wanted to have his palm read. I took his hand and made a few observations in a strange mixture of Greek and English. I can't imagine what he thought. A foreign woman holding his hand and muttering incomprehensibly to him.

After a while he gets up and goes out, only to return with a small bag of peanuts and a carnation. I look at Manolis. 'What does this mean?' I ask. He says, 'He wants you.' I say, 'I think I'm worth a little more than a bag of nuts.' He says, 'I will negotiate a price if you want.' I protest. I am not for sale, and anyway I thought, I was *his* woman. Upon which he says, 'You are alone and you have two children to look after, this man will pay you.' At that point I think I just went home but the man followed me around for weeks until I learnt to say, 'I don't want you,' in Greek and then he politely went away.

Then there was God. I was propositioned by God. There

were three men who came into the bar together some nights. One was a nice man who hired out scooters and spoke quite good English. The other was the man from the Customs House who spoke very good English in a very high-pitched voice. The third was an Orthodox priest who spoke no English but a little French. The scooter man was quite laid-back and clearly had no trouble attracting women if he wanted them. The Customs man never got a look in and was forever wanting to know why, in his squeaky voice, no woman wanted to have anything to do with him. But it was the priest who took a fancy to me.

As my Greek was still very limited and his English non-existent we resorted to French. God knows whether either of us understood very much of what was said but this was the gist of the conversation as I understood it. He opened by telling me that I might like to know that in Greece the priests could get married so they knew about women. I said, yes, I did know that. Then he went on to expound about the activities of the Greek boys with the tourist girls. He did not approve of that sort of thing. Oh right, that was important to know. But apparently, if I were to indulge him in anyway, that would be all right because it was tantamount to doing it with God. I said, 'But you're married, what about your wife?' Oh, that was all right, he assured me, she was asleep. I had difficulty not laughing out loud and I am afraid to tell you that I declined God's kind offer. I went home reflecting that only in Greece would a god have tried to seduce me.

And then, of course, there had to be a man called Odysseus, who told me he'd been waiting for me all his life. He didn't look like the Odysseus I had imagined and besides, he was married. They were all married. No young man over the age of twenty was free, but they all behaved as though they were, at least until the autumn rains appeared.

Come to think of it, the closest I got to a real god was a goatherd I met one day walking on the mountain behind the village. There was something about this man among the sage and the olive trees surrounded by goats and goat bells that really turned me on. It was like meeting Pan in his wild kingdom. Now that would have been a god worth sampling.

Meanwhile Persey had made a quick survey of the local talent and cast her net further afield. Desmond had been sent home. First of all she hooked up with a man from the American Air Force base on the island. He came with a friend who chatted me up for a while but I had more or less settled for Manolis at this point and he didn't look like a god to me. Besides I didn't really like being palmed off with the second choice. Again!

This first romance of Persey's didn't last very long and then she started sending for men by mail order. She was using an astrological dating agency so they should have come properly matched but that wasn't always the case. The first one to arrive had been in the army and was, I thought, slightly unhinged. I could hear him shouting orders to the children in the villa below and wasn't at all sure he was a safe person to have around. My response was to become a sort of surrogate man. I found myself challenging him to swimming contests and shouting louder.

'Shouting man' went away and was followed by some other strange creatures. Eventually, however, a rather nice chap called Alan turned up, a Taurean I think, and he seemed to fit the bill. He came, he went, he came back again and then suddenly they were on their way home and I was to be left with my two children and no particular plans for anything.

Not long before Persey left, I was walking near the village. I had taken a path along a slope beside a valley planted with olive trees. Stopping to look out across the valley I noticed a low wall made of large finished stones a few hundred yards from where I was standing. I made my way across. Yes, there it was, the first two courses of a rectangular building, probably a small temple. *THE SITE OF APHRODITE.*

Having found it we all assembled there, brought a few flowers and stones and made our individual offerings to the goddess. While we were doing this I noticed a buzzard overhead. It stayed above us for a while, perhaps hoping for a sacrifice, stooped a little and then flew away. Somewhere in the hills I heard the sound of goat bells. Persey must have thanked the goddess for finding the Taurean and they set off encouraged by the good omens.

That was late August and we could have left as well but I decided that we would stay, at least for the full year. The term was about to start again and Adam didn't want to go back to school, so I said, 'What the hell,' and we had three months in which just to be.

I took this opportunity to visit the sites which were off the beaten track. We drove to Lato where an ancient city still sits deserted above the modern town. In the spring it is full of wild flowers. Now it was dry and quiet and the altars deserted. We went into the mountains, to the plain of Lassithi where windmills stood like single blooms among the fields. Here, high in the mountains is the Dikteon Cave, the birthplace of Zeus.

I don't like going underground but I wasn't going to miss this experience.

We were taken into the cave by a guide, who carried Bun on his shoulders. We walked down rickety staircases and stone steps slippery with water into the deep dark underworld, the womb that gave birth to the Father of the Gods. Walking out I felt as though I was walking out into the birth of civilization, bringing memories of those first stirrings into the sunlight. Unlike Orpheus I did not look back in case William was following us and turning to look might send him tumbling back into the underworld. Driving back down the hairpin bends above the valleys we looked down on circling birds, on villages and little churches perched on hilltops. Then, for a bizarre moment, two dark grey fighter jets cruised past beneath us, like ancient furies.

We spent most afternoons on the beach. Evenings eating at the local taverna as the sun set over the autumn sea. Then next door to the bar to drink and dance before going home. I had become quite an expert in the matter of Greek dancing and took it upon myself to tutor the incoming tourists. Dancing was my form of sanity. I also occasionally manned the bar while Manolis went out on an errand, so I was quite a fixture.

Manolis didn't pay for these services, of course. Instead he offloaded the remaining stock from a small shop he used to run. I got tins of spam, jars of jam and bottles of wine, which I think he'd bottled himself. I had stacks of the things. So in the days before we left I sent the children round the village to distribute them. Aphrodite's offerings left on doorsteps and windowsills everywhere. No one asked them what they were doing. Some people didn't know who'd left them. They may still be there.

I don't know what I felt about my relationship with Manolis. He used to say to me, 'There are people who need looking after and people who look after them. You and me, we are the looking-afters.' I needed him there to remind me that ordinary life still went on. I think, for once, he had to make some kind of relationship with a woman other than the passing tourists. We were strange friends for a season. Perhaps we were looking after each other?

*Richard's wedding must be about now and I hope to hear all about it when I eventually get back to Mashad, which should certainly be no later than February/early March. I plan to be there before April so hope to get a piece of wedding cake so I can dream of my future husband!!*

# DEATH

*Cassandra: I screamed. I yelled. I ran into the Hilton Hotel and told them. Help, help. I need a doctor. I've hurt my hand. My hand was caught in the door. My hand is bleeding. Help me please. The man behind the desk called for a doctor. I wouldn't let him touch me. I couldn't bear to be touched. They wanted to call for the police. They said I was disturbing the guests. The doctor said they should send me to the asylum. I think he knew I wouldn't be safe with the police. He didn't know what else to do.*

*BROKEN*

One of our plans in Greece was to run some kind of course in personal enlightenment. Fed by myths of heroes, the journeys to the underworld and all the New Age stuff about clearing your past and moving forward, we thought up several strategies. Before we left we had a name. Our enterprise was to be called *The Chariot of the Sun*. Persey had designed a logo based on the Tarot image for *The Chariot*. I still have it somewhere among my personal possessions, a small metal stamp used by the printers. Of course now it would all be done online but in those days you still had to go to the print shop and the die was cast.

Once we were in the landscape we began to spot possibilities. There was a beach close by with huge pebbles rubbed smooth by the sea. They were of a size that would only fit comfortably in two cupped hands. We decided we would take our students down to the beach and tell them to weigh the stones until they found pebbles that matched their emotional relationships in life – good or bad. They would then be supplied with paints and asked to decorate them accordingly. Perhaps grandma's stone would be a cake, father's a briefcase, brother's a motorbike... or just a pattern, a Fabergé egg. Some of these relationships would be ones they valued, some they would be glad to get rid of. They would also be asked to pick a stone to represent themselves.

Having done all this wonderful artwork they would be asked to put the stones in a bag and carry them up the mountain where there was a deserted village for them to reach. It was a long way and the path was steep and stony. How long before they decided to leave some of their emotional baggage on the slopes? Would they even arrive at the top with the stone that represented themselves? We imagined little shrines all along the path.

In the deserted village they would be invited to find a solitary spot, possibly one of the deserted houses, where they could sit and contemplate the journey. Who had they left behind? Why had they left them behind? Would they be collecting them on the way back?

Finally everyone would be invited to meet up at the threshing floor, a stone circle in the centre of the village. Here they would tell their stories, explain what had happened to them on the journey and which stones they'd left and why? Here they would spread their emotions out to dry in the sun and thresh out the chaff.

In the event no one came. We put an ad in *The Guardian* and there were a couple of enquiries, but in the end we decided the only people on the course were ourselves. We needed to decide what was important to us before we went home to get on with the rest of our lives.

One of my stones was my brother. When my mother had her stroke he took over her affairs. We had divided the spoils so that he would have the farm and look after her and I would get any money that was left when she died. Very soon after we made this agreement I realized I should have had kept control of the money and I was paranoid about what he would do with it.

First thing I heard was that he'd sold the farm and bought a much bigger establishment where there would be room for our mother to be part of their household and be properly looked after. I found it quite unsettling to have the family home disappeared on me, but I wasn't there and he had taken responsibility.

Then there was a letter. He was going to come out and see me. I was quite touched to begin with. I thought he actually wanted to see if I was OK. He arrived, with his son, who was Adam's mate from early childhood. We had some pleasant days. It was spring and still quite cold but the boys played on the beach and we took a trip to the old leper colony on the island of Spinalonga and there were meals and some talk of home.

Then he suddenly produced a map of his new place. It was a house in a valley with about three hundred acres. Most of the land belonged to the house but there was a small portion, including a cottage, which must have been sold out at some point. Instead of borrowing from the bank he wanted to know if he could use part of mother's money to buy the land. I would own it and he'd pay me rent. I might also like to buy the cottage when I came home.

At the time the rent for the land sounded like quite a lot of money as I have always been neurotic about earning enough to live on. For a moment I was quite taken with the idea and went to tell Persey. She was on the terrace half-naked and ironing at the time. She looked up at me and said, 'Why don't you just give it all to him right now? It's what he wants and then you won't have to think about it anymore?' I realized I would be relinquishing all control over my inheritance if I agreed.

I was furious. I walked the villa all night ready to kill.

In the end I simply said I was not going to take him up on his kind offer. That I realized, like Jason, it was not a good idea to give care of the Golden Fleece to the dragon and expect him to give it back at some later date. My brother was most hurt I should suggest any such thing but I know, and he knows, nothing good would have come of it. So that was a stone I might, or might not, have carried up the mountain.

I think about the stones I never painted. What would I paint on them now? I think of the weight in my hand. Their hold over me.

For my father, a picture of him in his army uniform – a wonderful blue silk tunic, white britches, black boots, a turban, a sash and a sword. I used to occasionally put the jacket on and parade about the house in it. Think it drove him mad. Also a picture I have of him standing on a chair in a little lacy dress at about the age of two. A photo of him holding me as a baby. He had only just come back from fighting in Burma. How odd it must have been for him. His medals. A bottle of whiskey. His horses. His guns.

For mother, her horses, her farm, the photo of my ayah holding me as a baby, the photo of her holding me. My grandmother's house, the house we came home to. Flowers from the garden where we both played as children. The paper hats she made for Adam and his cousin. The books she read to all of us.

For Charlotte, her old Afghan coat with the torn pocket. The document saying she was a Muslim. Her prayer mat. A picture of her jumping her pony at a horse show. The silver earrings she brought me from India. The little Chinese dragon which sits on the windowsill in my bedroom. And colour. Lots of colours. I wore her patchwork shirt for years after she had died.

For my brother Charlie, the little red wagon he used to

take with him everywhere when he was a child. The dogs he loved. The big house he always wanted to live in. The expensive cars he liked to drive even when he couldn't afford them. His children. His grandchildren.

For William, how could I paint a stone for him when he has painted so many for himself? But then of course I wrote a play about him. I have written plays about all of them. Those are my stones.

And for Persey, the Cretan snake goddess she bought for herself and left to me. A strange primitive figure she gave me the Christmas we were still in Crete. The stacked heels and tiny shorts she insisted on wearing. The eyes of the men that followed her everywhere. The eye of Athena's owl. Her dogs, her children, her grandchildren and the games she created for them. I could go on and on. But then this is her stone. You are holding it in your hand.

'She told me she was raped,' I say.

'You what?'

We are on the balcony of Persey's villa. The sun is splitting the stones. I am sitting on a plastic chair. Persey is lying naked on a towel. Brown all over. I notice the man next door has been watering his garden for a very long time. At this rate his precious water tank will soon be empty.

'She told me. I can't remember when. Must have been before that last phone call. She said she had been on the way to Mecca. She wanted to perform Haj. She met some men. Four men. They said they would take her there. They all piled into a taxi. Not to go to Mecca obviously. To go somewhere. And they raped her.'

'Oh my god. You didn't tell me this before,' says Persey.

'Not sure anyone believed her to begin with. She used to make up stories all the time.'

'Why on earth would she make up a story like that?'

'She said her hand was caught in the door. Her hand

101

was hurting. She kept wanting it to be over so she could get her hand back.'

'Did you believe her?'

'I believed her about the hand.'

'And the rape?'

'Yes, I believed her. But what could I do about it? I wasn't there.'

---

*Must get going as I don't feel I can accept the hospitality of this hotel for more than two nights (three is the maximum). And there is always more to do and see than I have time for. Between you, you and Daddy, you gave me everything I could ask for to equip me for the life I love to lead EXCEPT for language aptitude. My Iranian (Persian) is still atrocious despite the fact that I rarely converse in anything else. Well, no, that's not exactly true. The educated people with whom I have academic discussions speak excellent English but in the outback and the desert towns there aren't too many of those.*

---

# TEMPERANCE

*Cassandra: I was dead. Those men had taken something. Something I would never get back. I was walking in the desert. Looking. Trying to find her. Trying to bring her back home. But I knew she was gone. She was dead. Dead and buried. And then I find I have a gun in my hand. I knew I could find her then. I knew where she was... I take it out into the night. Out into the moonlight. But there is no moon. Out into the dark... I reach for the trigger with that hand. The hand that caught in the door. The hand that would have touched the stone. I... And my hand didn't hurt any more... I am a pilgrim. I am a child of god. Allah will look after me...*

*BROKEN*

I suppose Persey and I could have made a life in Crete if we had been more flexible but bringing our cars had made this very difficult. While we looked like tourists nobody bothered us, but if we got jobs the cars would have been impounded and there would have been import tax to pay. Just by having them we were almost forced to return. In those days Greece was not part of the European Union.

At one point we thought we would retire to France where the property was still cheap and the children would be properly educated. We located an agent and were sent details of a few properties and I was delegated to go and see them. I hired a car at the airport and headed for the town where the agent was located.

Arriving with slightly more French than Greek I did my best to make myself understood. The agent was most obliging and I spent the morning stumbling along until at lunch time as we returned to the office she asked,

'Would you rather we spoke in English?' and I realized I had probably been invisible on every subject for most of the day. Can't remember whether it was a Thursday or not.

The houses were lovely but I think it began to dawn on me that, as a writer, I was not being properly fed in places where the language was not mine. But I did take the opportunity to go and visit William's grave. Here I found a mound strewn with stones and a roughly hammered piece of brass which said, *'Love echoes through the universe'*, and some plastic flowers that could have been left by a child.

I bought a picture from his gallery. The blue angel. And on his grave I left a dolphin ring I had bought in Crete and wished him safe journey wherever he was. Another stone had been carried up a mountain.

I came back and pronounced on the houses. Persey settled for her Taurean and departed. I decided to wait till the end of the year. And then we were also on our way home. I packed everything we owned in the back of the car, said goodbye to the cats and the landlord and set out for the ferry at Iraklion. At least this time when they gave me directions for parking I knew what they were saying. We arrived in Piraeus and set out to drive to the ferry for Italy. On the way I wanted to visit Mycenae, but Adam was feeling ill, so we drove on, found a place to stay and had our last Greek meal on the quayside.

On the boat to Italy I realised I hadn't brought enough money to pay for supper, so we shared one meal. Arriving late in the evening, our first port of call was a pizzeria and we then set out north with no real idea of where we would spend the night. As we drove into the gathering gloom we could see the lights of villages high in the mountains and eventually headed for one. I couldn't make myself understood in Italian – not even to say I was 'invisible' – so we all went to sleep in the car.

Everything was going very well until I pulled out of a petrol station on to a motorway and the car came to a halt and I couldn't start it again. I can't remember how we got into to town, but someone must have towed us to a garage and the owner recommended a hotel. I was running now on some money which had landed in my bank account from a cottage which had belonged to my grandmother's gardener and sold to accommodate an expanding new town. I have to say that all my life, although I've lived as carefully as I could, there have been little pots of money planted along the way and discovered just when I need them. This was to help us find a house in England when we got home.

We stayed in a small town just outside Florence and spent our days exploring Renaissance treasures and buying wonderful Italian ice creams. The car seemed to be taking forever to mend – parts to source, mechanics to find, public holidays. I did wonder if we would ever get home. And then the news came that the car was ready and I paid my hotel bill. Wouldn't it be a day on which all the taxi drivers were on strike? I was ready to scream but, of course, the hotel manager said he would take us to the garage. More Italian kindness.

And then we get home. I hadn't let my brother know we were coming. I have never been to his new house. We turn into a long private road which seems to go on forever. We turn a corner to see a large house with a Range Rover parked outside. Everyone looks a bit taken aback, including my mother, who has to be told who we are. We stay the night in a room in my mother's part of the house and I take the chance to have a look at the cottage next door which my brother had wanted me to buy. It seems like a nice enough place but my instinct tells me to get as far away as I can if I am ever to feel I have a life of my own.

My intended destination was East Anglia. Whilst in Greece I had read an article in *The Guardian* about a healer called Matthew Manning, who lived in Bury St Edmunds. I wanted to know what that was all about, so we set out for Ipswich where I had a school friend. I bowled up in my car with the two boys and everything we owned in the world piled in the back. I could see by her face she thought she might have us for several months but when I set out the next day I said, 'I won't come back this evening unless I've found a house.' Yes, right!

I had sent for house details while in Greece and wandered around looking at some of these. Towards evening we arrived in Debenham where there was a house for sale on the edge of the churchyard. Since I had an ongoing relationship with dead people I thought this might be a good resting place. Also the children would have somewhere to play which didn't involve me doing any gardening. In the event the agent told me the house was already under offer, so I began to think we might have to sleep in a haystack or go back to my friend – defeated.

We went into a tea room where I asked the owner if she knew of any houses that were for rent. Perhaps buying a house in one day was a bit ambitious? She said they had just bought another house in the neighbouring village of Eye and her husband might very well be willing to rent out the upstairs, while they ran the downstairs as a restaurant.

We waited. Her husband appeared. Turned out he was a man of Indian extraction and he was very happy to take us over to see the house. On the way he said he didn't really want to have to rent part of it out, he would rather sell it. We arrived in the dark and looked round. It was a beautiful 16th century beamed farmhouse, already converted into a restaurant. When I was in Greece and thinking of coming home I had made a wish list which included furniture, as I

106

had sold what we had when we left, a fitted carpet and central heating. Here we had four bedrooms, all furnished, fitted carpets and a form of central heating.

Only trouble was the carpets sported a dreadful floral pattern and the central heating was solid fuel which I never really mastered. Still, it was a house, it was furnished and it was empty. It also offered me a way of earning a living, although that didn't figure at the time. What really sold me on it was a big red brick Victorian workshop in the yard outside with huge windows and a couple of stables. There seemed to be a vast amount of property for the price.

On the way back to Debenham Adam asked our host where he had come from in India? I could sense a feeling of resistance. How many times had he been asked this? I explained that Adam wasn't being rude. I had been born in India and he was curious.

'Oh where?' he asks.

'Mussoorie' I say, 'a small hill station north of Delhi.'

He pulls the car to a halt. 'I come from just down the road,' he says, 'from Dehra Dun. I walk up to Mussoorie to shoot game.'

'Oh,' I add, 'and my mother lived in Dehra Dun. She only went to Mussoorie because there was a hospital up there.'

So here I was being offered a house by a man who came from the place where I was born. If I was on a mythical journey this had to be a significant moment. There could only be one outcome. I was able to go back to my friend that evening with a clear conscience.

---

*Today I found the most beautiful prayer rug in the Bazaar. Of course I couldn't afford it (all the more reason to buy it). It was sitting in a shoe mender's shop. Asked him if he wanted to sell it, he gave me a price (around £7.50) so I bought it. In the bank later was offered twice that immediately by the most charming orthopaedic surgeon who was also waiting to see the manager in his office, and it was much admired in the mosque. It's between 80–100 years old.*

---

# THE GATEKEEPER

*Cassandra: I climbed over the barbed wire fence. My coat caught. It was heavy with rain. I had to put the gun down. My coat was torn. If death was my lover he would take me with a torn coat. I wondered who would find me? I thought of mother asleep at the farm. She would get up early. Go out and talk to her animals. She only ever really talked to her animals. Of Diana asleep with her child in Ireland. Of Jason asleep with his family. Everyone asleep. And then I thought, no more waking in the dark and wondering. No more struggling to get free. No more pain. No more words. It was a quiet place. Death for me was a quiet place. A moment of wild thunder and then silence. Perhaps Death is the lover Di is waiting for... If so, I'll have him first.*

*BROKEN*

The Dove House Tea Rooms turned out to be a great idea. I got to know everyone in the town very quickly and the boys learnt how to clear tables. I found people to help me with the cooking and they became great friends. Mind you, they wouldn't let me in the kitchen during business hours unless it was to do the washing up. I was strictly front-of-house which suited me fine. We had a very steady lunch clientele from the local businesses and the man from the pub helped us out with change and sent warning telephone calls when the Health and Safety Inspector was on the way. The only problem was that I hardly ever saw daylight. Tuesdays was the only day we were closed and on those days I had to go to the Cash-and-Carry. I was going slightly nuts.

After about three years I decided to renovate the barn at the back and rent the tea rooms out. I was going to write

109

full-time and hoped that the eventual sale of the tea rooms would pay for everything. It was a wonderful building which we had used as an art gallery and a place for the children to play. At one point they knocked a hole in the back wall and took to running along the walls of neighbouring gardens like cats. I think the year in Greece had given them a sense in which whole world was an adventure playground and nobody seemed to mind.

To begin with the barn was also inhabited by a large solitary rat, who we christened Roland. Occasionally I would spot what looked like a cat running across the yard, only to realise it was in fact our personal rodent. For a while another friend, Colin, took up residence in the barn. He had some money coming to him and was waiting to make a trip to India. He made a space for himself at the end of the barn and settled in. One night he woke to hear the sound of something bumping along the wooden floor in the main part of the building. Roland then appeared at the end of his bed dragging a large potato from the vegetable store downstairs and retreated behind his suitcase to consume it. There was a lot of scrabbling and bits of potato appearing above the suitcase, from which he concluded that Roland probably hadn't got many teeth left.

On another occasion, late into the winter, Colin bought a survival blanket to help him keep warm, one of those things made out of silver foil which they wrap athletes in after a marathon. He woke one morning to find the blanket had gone. Investigation revealed that Roland had stolen it, chewed it up and made a nest for himself behind the suitcase. I think it was about this time that Colin got his money and moved to warmer climes. Shortly after that I started the renovation.

While all this was going on I wouldn't like you to think I had given up on William. I talked to him all the time and spent the odd evening trying to conjure him in my own reflection in the mirror. After a while I found that if I stopped straining for his features and just relaxed the image began to change and all sorts of faces came through. A young man with curly hair, an old woman, lots of strangers.

I decided then it might be better to engage a professional. My first port of call was to phone one of the Spiritualist churches in Ipswich. Did they have anyone who could act as medium? They gave me a couple of names. I chose one and made an appointment.

I followed instructions, turning left off the Norwich Road into a pattern of streets lined with 1930's semis. I stopped the car. I was early. I waited and watched the world go by. An elderly man coming back from the corner shop with a paper and some milk. A young woman with a child in a pushchair struggling to negotiate a stiff gate. Everyone getting on with ordinary life. I found I was quite nervous.

The time arrived. I got out of the car and walked up a short, paved path to the front door. I rang the bell. I waited. I saw a shadow against the frosted glass. The shadow disappeared for a moment and then reappeared. The door opened. A nice, middle-aged woman stood in front of me holding a snake. Well, not a real snake, that would have been something. A stuffed snake of the woollen variety that was obviously used as a draught excluder. 'Come in,' she said kindly – the woman, not the snake – and I followed her into the kitchen where she put the snake down on the table and offered me a cup of tea. I accepted.

Later we are in the sitting room. She in an armchair. Me on the sofa. The tea on a small table between us.

'Have you brought anything with you that might help me connect?' she asks. I handed her one of William's pictures wrapped in a brown paper bag. 'Is it a picture?'

It was. It was the painting of a man dressed in a

medieval costume. A falconer. It came from a series of paintings called *Medieval Images* which related to his time in Conques.

I say, 'Yes.' She says she will look at it later. I am relieved. I don't want her reading anything into it.

She sits for a while with the package on her lap. I try to empty my mind so that what she says won't come directly from me. I become very aware of her pink, fluffy slippers and want to laugh. William would certainly be laughing at me. I wonder if he even knows where Ipswich is?

'I see a man,' she says. 'He's laughing. Brown, curly hair. Blue eyes. He's dressed up in some kind of protective clothing. Like cricket pads. I think he's saying you are well-protected.'

This wasn't William. His hair was black and straight and his eyes were brown. Could have been my father I supposed. Although I couldn't imagine him wanting to contact me. I was still very angry with him. A situation not to be resolved for another twenty years. Then perhaps it was him. Perhaps he'd come suitably protected from my wrath.

I didn't say anything. I didn't want to give her any clues.

She talked on. I don't remember much of it. It didn't seem to be particularly relevant. But then there was a moment when she flinched. 'A car crash. He died in a car. That wasn't very nice. He didn't mean to die, he says. He meant to stay with you. Does that make any sense?' I said it did. It was the only thing that made sense so far. But I was losing faith by then.

But then. Just before the end. Her face lit up. 'Ah,' she says, 'now here's someone who's keen to see you. A man dressed in a flat cap and waistcoat and a shirt with no collar. There's string round the bottom of his trousers and a spade in his hand. A working man. Do you know who it is?'

I think of my grandmother's gardener, of a man who

112

used to help my mother look after her horses. It could be either of them.'

'He's taking his cap off to you. He says you've done well. And he's looking out for you still. I'm getting a name. Wait a minute.'

She shuts her eyes. I wait. 'Alf, his name is Alf. Does that mean anything to you?'

'Oh yes,' I speak at last. 'That is my grandmother's gardener. I used to follow him around everywhere. I was two-years-old. He must've have found me a bit of a nuisance, but he was very kind.'

'Well, he's still looking out for you.'

That made more sense to me than anything else she'd said before. I sat thinking about the garden that we'd come home to. Of the lawn and the oak and the weeping ash where I hid from the world. Filling the mobile water butt from the pump. Following the trail of water as Alf moved it along the asphalt paths to the walled garden. The smell of box hedges. Figs and peaches ripening in the sun. Asparagus ferns moving like seaweed in the wind. Alf moving among them like a creature from the deep.'

'Well, there you are,' she says. 'I don't think I can give you any more.'

She looks at the picture. She tells me she lost her own husband in a bizarre accident. He had gone out to work one morning and never come back. 'I felt it. I felt it in my bones but I didn't know what had happened. He was going round a roundabout behind a lorry loaded with wood. The load came loose and went straight through the windscreen and beheaded him. Not the sort of thing you expect. But I knew. Of course I still hear from him. I write it down, what he says to me. We both did automatic writing when he was alive, so I was well prepared. Still, you don't get over it do you? Not really.'

I sympathise. I thank her. I leave. The street outside seems faintly unreal but otherwise just the same. I feel strangely dissatisfied. I don't feel I've really heard from William, but I have heard from Alf. He was the last person on my mind so perhaps this is proof of something? It was Alf's cottage which was sold to provide me with the house I had now. Who'd have thought Alf would be my benefactor?

During this time Persey went through several lifetimes. First of all she'd gone back to London to live with the Taurean. Then, for reasons I never quite understood, she bought a huge house in Italy which was more or less falling down. There were floors upstairs that could not be walked on. Floors that you could see right through. There was no running water, only water tanks which were shared with the local wildlife, including snakes. There was wood to collect, food to grow, a road to build. The boys tell me they spent an inordinate amount of time setting stones and they were all terrified of the snakes. I think one day the money ran out and they just left. This time she left the green car at Pisa airport with the keys in it. It wasn't worth bringing home and for the car Italy was home.

Then she went to France. The Taurean and some friends bought a derelict French village to create a kind of holiday resort and Persey went out to supervise the renovation. She employed local builders to do the really heavy work but she must have done huge amounts herself, certainly most of the decorating. She had bought a house nearby so she and the boys settled in and, for a while, the boys went to school.

We lost touch through most of this time, I think because I wanted to settle down where I was. The trip to Greece had shaken my sense of security and I thought Eye was a good place for the boys to go to school and for us to belong to a community. I think there was one phone call, in which

Persey said she was thinking of going back to Greece and asked if I wanted to come, but I wasn't going to repeat that experience.

---

*It was very cold today, bitter winds in the afternoon and I got very angry with the women in the mosque. A male friend followed me when I stormed out before the sermon and when he asked me why I was cross I told him that I had EARNED my right to pray with the men. In fact had thought of moving that afternoon, before evening prayers, but had to stay for various reasons. But if another mosque insists (and none has before although they held up prayers for five minutes once in the Holiest and oldest Mosque in Isfahan considering the issue) I will go out without offering prayers. The women are very holy and very concerned for my welfare – they said smoking was bad for me — but they seem to be without that dry, biting sense of humour I love so in the Arabic men.*

---

# THE TOWER

*Explains everything. The wait. The feeling I had that I couldn't leave. The moment of recognition when I first met my child's father. The intimations of meaning that have escaped me. I know what it is to be deserted. Why I was deserted. But I also know that desertion bears a different kind of fruit. Amelia made her silver amulets and sold them. People came from miles around to buy them. Eventually she did not have to pretend they contained the remains of the saint. It was enough that she made them. She grew to love her work as I love mine. As she loved Francis. A way of making perfect in an imperfect world. And she loved her son who loved her. And when she died she knew the value of every little thing that had gone to make her life. Went quiet to her grave. Francis only knew as he died. And then only what he'd lost.*

SHADOWS IN THE DOORWAY

The next attempt at spiritual exploration was to see if I could make contact with a past life. I was at a party talking to a hypnotherapist friend and asked if she knew anyone who took people back into past lives. She said she could do it, just no one ever asked her. We made an appointment.

When I arrived she asked me if there was anything in particular I wanted to look at. Of course I wanted to know if William and I had been together in a past life but I didn't particularly want to specify this, as it might lead to wish fulfilment rather than a true experience. So I said, 'No.'

She asks me to lie on a bed, relax and imagine I am floating high above the earth. To come down when I feel drawn to a particular place. I float for a while surveying various landscapes and then find myself coming down in a place which is very familiar. I am back on my hill in Kent

116

descending into the valley where I had walked so often. I am slightly off my usual circuit near another church. I remember seeing signs of strip farming and talk of the village moving further up the hill at the time of the Black Death.

This must be earlier. The village is still there. It is a simple place. Roughly thatched huts. Chickens and pigs rooting in the dirt. Children. I am in a hut. There is a bed made of sticks and some kind of cloth. There is a central firepit and a few things hung from the rafters. I don't seem to find much of interest. My friend tells me to move forward in time.

I am still in the hut, but this time I am shaking. At first I think it is the sound of men arriving on horseback but then I realise it is me. I am lying on the bed and I am shaking. I am ill. I am dying. There is a man standing at the door watching, an older woman sitting by the smoking fire. I assume the man is my husband but he doesn't seem that bothered about what's happening to me. I get a feeling he is waiting for it to be over so he can get on with feeding the pigs.

I die. I float off. My friend suggests I find another place to go. This time I find myself coming down over Conques. *Oh well,* I think, *I might as well find out what happened here.*

Not unsurprisingly I arrive in the studio, the house where I had stayed. I am standing at the window looking down into the square. It is filled with people. Rich people, dressed in velvet and brocade and heavy with jewellery. I can't think why there are so many and then it dawns. This is a place of pilgrimage. These are pilgrims come to establish their right to a place in heaven.

I watch for a while. Then I can see myself. I am dressed almost as well as they are. A red velvet outfit, rather like

117

the one in William's picture of *The Falconer*. Jewels in my hat. Rings on my fingers. But I am no pilgrim. I am preying on them. Selling them relics. As a child I had tended the goats on the mountainside, collected bones and other little treasures, which were now being presented as bones of the saint, cloth from her robes, even slivers of the True Cross. I have them set into silver rings and amulets. These people, who are so hungry for heaven, are making me rich. I laugh out loud.

Now, I am moving out of the square, down a hill. There are houses perched like birds' nests on the edge of the mountain. I stop outside one of them. I don't want to go in. I am overcome with emotion. I move so I can see in. There is a woman with her back to me working close to a window which looks out over the valley. There was so much love in this room, but I know I'm not going to stay. She is the woman who makes the jewellery for me. I love her. Her love for me is palpable. But I know that if I stay in this room with her I will never go out into the world, never leave this place, and I want to make more of myself.

She turns. She is pleading with me to stay. I leave. I walk back into the sunlight knowing I am never coming back. But the person who walks away is just a suit of clothes, an empty shell. I have left something of myself behind in this little house on the hill.

Then I am much older. I am in a garden. It is night-time. I am standing by a pond looking up at the stars and remembering the girl I left behind. Somewhere in the background there is a party going on. It is my daughter's wedding day. I had left the mountain and gone to the valleys where there were men who could afford gold for their reliquaries. I had found a man who worked gold as well as silver and I had made my fortune. I invested it in cattle and land and married a girl who was also well-appointed. We have children, a boy and a girl, and the girl is marrying another man with land and money. I have accomplished everything I set out to do, but I still feel empty. I am big and well-fed and still very richly dressed, wearing a much bigger version of my red suit. I say, 'I am an empty thing and full of sorrow. I have grown so large to accommodate my grief.'

And now I am shaking. I know this shaking from the first life. I am dying. I do die. I leave this body and float off towards the mountains where I find the girl I left behind. She has gone on making her jewellery without the relics and made quite a reputation for herself. People come to buy her work because she makes it, not because it is blessed by the presence of the saint. She also has a son, my son, who she has brought up on her own. I had abandoned both of them.

Coming back from this session I felt I had been given a revelation. The child I had abandoned was William. I remembered him saying the saint had spoken to him, called him 'my little angel'. This time he had abandoned me.

I was high as a kite for weeks. And I wanted more. In the meantime I wrote a play, *Shadows in the Doorway*, which was produced by BBC Radio 4 and waited for the next revelation. This came much later.

---

*My plans are now drastically altered (since getting back here this evening ) but I won't tell you about them until and if they materialize because it's no good getting overexcited about things, as I now am, as it usually messes things up – like it did that night that Daddy went to London and we had such a dreadful row after so looking forward to a quiet evening together.*

*But I hope you haven't forgotten the long spells when we got on so well together before my conversion. And I'm sorry about all that you had to put up with when I came home after my first Islamic excursion.*

119

*You know, it's really hard to become a real Moslem in your own right, especially if you're a woman receiving and demanding the rights of a man, and I could never believe when in England that Islam is so incredible. At least I can be wholly and totally me here, and it was as though the Moslem faith has always been that of my heart. Also the architecture, the carpets, the copperwork – all the crafts, in fact, which you see going on in the Bazaars and which the fathers begin to teach their sons when they are about five. And in the mosques (perhaps especially there) there is none of this holiness shit – prayers are offered to Allah only and after prayers if you feel like a chat and a smoke then that's what you get into.*

---

# THE STAR

*Isobel: It's all over. Gone. I saw it in their eyes. Pity. Embarrassment. Fear it might happen to them. I couldn't understand half of what they said. God knows what words came out when I opened my mouth. When I was sitting in the pew and they came to talk to me I noticed they bent down. Like you do to a child or a cripple of an old woman who has lost her sense. Even my best friend spoke to me like an idiot. That tone. A dreadful combination of common sense and enforced kindness. Nurse speak...*

*MOTHERING SUNDAY*

Then, right out of the blue, I got a phone call from Persey's mother. Persey had had an accident in France and was lucky to be alive, as was her youngest son, Oliver, who was in the car with her. She had been unconscious for several weeks and was now back in England in hospital and would I go and see her? I had nearly lost someone else in a French car crash. I went.

I arrived in a private hospital near Canterbury and had to don protective clothing as Persey had contracted MRSA. She told me of extraordinary visions she'd had as she lay in her coma. Being escorted through mythical landscapes by a Pan-like figure who made her feel protected and cared for. She said she might never have returned if Oliver hadn't been there to talk her back.

Her injuries were fairly horrific. Her face had been badly damaged and had to be partially reconstructed. She also had a broken arm which had been pinned and broken ribs which came very close to puncturing her heart. She had been a whisker away from arriving in the underworld and I found myself experiencing a pang of jealousy thinking she

121

might have seen William before me. I didn't entirely trust either of them in this world or the next.

By this stage it was difficult to know quite what held us together. This wasn't an easy relationship. She was much more sexually relaxed than me and I was often jealous, or just resentful because of the fact that I felt I had to protect her from her worst choices. I remembered that conversation in her kitchen all those years ago, and thought perhaps she had indeed moved into the space left by my sister which she had said might be a fatal place to stand. But Persey clearly had no intention of going anywhere. She recovered enough to rent a house in Canterbury and gather her children around her again.

Shortly after this my mother died and I had money and new choices to make.

My mother had lived with my brother and sister-in-law for most of the nine years, but recently she had turned her face to the wall and my sister-in-law had had enough. So they found her a nursing home nearby.

The boys and I went down to visit her once and found her sitting in a room with lots of other old people watching endless television and being addressed by her first name, something she would never have sanctioned. We stayed for a bit. The tea was brought. Mother stole food off all the nearest plates. And we went home. One thing I did discover was that no one had told the nursing home I existed, so I left my name and number. Another form of invisibility.

Not long after my brother and his family went to America for the Christmas holiday. They had not been able to go away as a family for nine years. The plane can hardly have landed when the nursing home rang me up. My mother wasn't well and they were worried. I left my boys with some friends and drove to Kent. When I walked into the room she recognised me. I saw death on her face and I knew she didn't really want to be here. But she was strong. She was hanging on. And I went home.

Two days later another phone call. I was back in the car. When I got there this time she was quietly fading away. She knew me. I told her we were all alright, my brother and I, and she could go if she wanted. I knew my brother should have been there but it occurred to me that she had arranged it like this so I would see her out. I remember thinking, *I am the first born, this is my job*, and it healed whatever rift it was that had kept me away from her.

That night I stayed with some friends nearby, still not sure if this was the end. During the evening I felt her presence very strongly in the room. 'She's here, she's come to say goodbye,' I said. And we went on with our evening.

The next morning we sat over breakfast and I was late leaving. On the way I had another visitation. My mother was driving the car for me. I could feel her there. When I arrived at the home there was a bit of a panic on. The nurse had seen her first thing, gone to get her a cup of tea and when she came back she had quietly slipped away.

She was still warm when I went in and looked incredibly peaceful, as though she was sleeping. I opened the window to let her spirit out. It was a gorgeous winter's morning. A hunting morning. I imagined father waiting for her with the horses. I said, 'Pop's got the horses ready, you can go.'

I looked round for ritual elements. I had earth and air and there was water in the tap. I wished I'd brought a candle. Just then, under the window, the bursar emerged with a couple of cardboard boxes and set light to an enormous bonfire. Now we had fire.

Later, I realised, she had been in the nursing home almost nine months to the day. Another form of gestation.

My brother and his family came home. We had a bit of

a service and a huge row over the will. We didn't speak to each other again for twelve years. But I still had plenty of money to make other choices.

---

*I must mend my coat. It's cold and I have a long day tomorrow, if all goes to plan, so will sign off now. Might not write again until I get to Mashad but current plans make that probably sooner rather than later i.e. around early February and if current plans materialize. I could not be permitted to say a great deal about them to a non-Moslem. Only here, unlike England, they encourage you to overreach yourself and are kind and helpful when you've overdone it. Like if the 'A' level episode at Ashford Tech. had happened here they'd have seen that I had the facilities and tuition to do the science for medicine in half the time because Allah and Akbar (Allah is greater), always encourages and help from those able to give it because your honest best is honourable and to discourage or prohibit that would be against the natural order of Islam.*

*Am rabbiting, the reason being that I don't feel like mending my coat and am not tired.*

*Please give all my love to all the family. Hope that all is going well on the farm and that you're having a good hunting season.*

*With lots of love,*
*Saarah xx*

---

# THE MOON

*Isobel: What did I feel when my mother began to go down?*
*I don't think I ever relied on her much. Father was the*
*rock. She was a butterfly in blue. She faded. Ever so*
*gently. She didn't bring us up. We had a nanny, Nanny*
*Peters. A bit fierce but we were fond of her. She'd tell*
*me to get on with it. To cope as usual. Suppose I can.*
*Resign myself to being a silly old bat until the day I can*
*escape them all forever. They won't notice whether I'm*
*here or not as long as I have my body draped about the*
*place for them to tend. I can go anywhere. Back to the*
*mountains. To those moments at dawn when I sat*
*outside the tent and saw the sun rise over the rim of the*
*world.*

*MOTHERING SUNDAY*

Adam was at boarding school in Woodbridge and I
suddenly felt that if I didn't spend time with him before he
left school I would lose him forever. I had done up the barn
at the back of the house and never expected to leave it, but
now I had my mother's money and other choices to make.
I started looking for houses.

I had made a couple of trips to the town and seen a few
houses and then Persey turned up again. A new set of house
details arrived that morning in the post. A Victorian semi,
very close to the centre of town, with four bedrooms. It
looked as though it might be the answer.

We collected the key from the estate agents and went to
see it. I liked it. It was in a nice quiet street and the house
seemed to be a fairly good nick with quite a few 'period
features'. Its only real drawback was that the living room
was almost entirely blue. Blue carpet, blue walls, a blue
ceiling, even the light bulbs were blue. But there were four

125

good-sized bedrooms, including a large attic, and a long garden with a shed. Persey was quite sure this was the right place for me. More to the point it had just been reduced in price by a considerable amount and it was empty. We were in the middle of a housing slump.

Arriving back at the estate agents I said I was interested, only to be told an offer had already been made. If I had been on my own I might have walked away but Persey looked very hard at the receptionist and said, 'Oh, is this a new sales technique? We thought you were an estate agent and sold houses. Now, we're going out to find a cup of tea and when we come back we want to see the man in charge and my friend here might bother to buy a house off you.'

We returned to be shown into the inner office and I offered the asking price. This seemed to do the trick.

Leaving my newly-reconstructed barn was heart-breaking. Friends turned up to beg me not go, but I had learnt not to ignore these promptings from the cosmos. As it was things could not have turned out better. The house brought all of us up and I was still there twenty-five years later.

Later I discovered there was a footnote to the move that surprised even me. Family research revealed that my great-great grandfather had been vicar in a village five miles away from Woodbridge and his son and his nephew-in-law and several great-uncles had lived round there for all of their lives. I had in fact come home.

About this time Persey decided to change her name. I think she felt that one visit to the underworld, however fascinating, was quite enough. From then on she wanted to be called 'Lucia' and belong in the light. It took me quite some time to be comfortable with this new name, but then Persephone hadn't been her given name either so why not?

She also decided to choose her own surname. This time

she chose 'Carina', after a mass of stars that belong to the constellation Argos Navis, named after the ship on which Jason sailed in his quest for the Golden Fleece. She was on another journey, this time in the heavens above.

When we moved Bun also changed his name. From now on he was called Will.

---

### My last letter from Charlotte – or what I remember of it – February 1977

*Dear Peps,*

*I am in a strange place. Thought I ought to let someone know. But you don't need to do anything. I am safe and I am happy. Perhaps happier than I have been for a long time. I am in a lunatic asylum in Cairo. Have been here for about a week. Met a man in Mashad who was coming this way and I thought, why not? Bummed around in Cairo. Saw the Pyramids. Rode a camel. Usual things. Then met a man in a café... went round town. Talked. Smoked. Ended up in the Hilton Hotel where I decided to vent my feelings about England and Christianity and how no one was doing anything to make it right. Apparently I was shouting at their precious customers and taking off my clothes. Manager sent for the police but the boy I was with rang his father – some high up man in the government – and he said not to let the police get hold of me. Send me to the bin...*

---

# THE SUN

**Tom:** *Over the top. Follow the flash. Don't stop for anything. That's what they told us. Just keep moving. Just keep on. If the man in front of you falls. Step on him. There'll be men behind you. Following you. You can't stop. Or Jerry'll know he can beat us.*

*I was right behind you, Percy. Right on your tail. Knew while I could see you there was something, someone still alive. Tried to catch up with you. Running to catch up with you. Mud pulling at my feet. Bullets singing in the air. Flash flashing. Men falling round us like fruit. I was nearly there. Then woof and a crash and you're gone.*

*I stopped. They told us not to stop. I stopped. Couldn't believe me eyes. Just stood there looking at the hole where you'd been. And then you were there. Buried in the mud. And I was down there with you. Digging to get you out. Bits of you everywhere. All down the front of me. Blood in my lap. All down me legs. Blood and mud and bits.*

*Shaking. You were shaking. Kept saying, 'Hold me Tom, just hold me.' Held on all right, hard as I bloody could. Held you. Held you close. Closer than I've held anyone. Even my Mary.*

*And then you went quiet. And smiled. I thought. He's OK. He's going to be all right. And then you said, 'Don't wait around here for too long mate, best beer's in the pub over the road.'*

*Oh god, man, what I am I going to do without you? You cheerful fucking bastard... what am I going to tell your Silvie?*

*ALWAYS THE GUNS*

So I moved to Woodbridge and began the strangest part of my mythical journey.

I was working on a commissioned play about the discovery of the Sutton Hoo treasure in 1939. The landowner, Mrs Pretty, who paid for the dig, was a great believer in spiritualism and went to London to consult with her dead husband every Thursday. Clearly I had to find out a bit more about how this worked. And, of course, I was interested to see if any of my dead friends and relatives were ready to speak to me. I found a Spiritualist Church and took Will with me, partly on the off-chance his father would have something to say to him.

The first session was hilarious. It involved people wanting to know where they'd left bits of jewellery and whether the man would arrive to mend the washing machine. The medium was really quite impressive. He certainly seemed to have a line open to their needs. But the communication which really did for us was a woman who got messages from her dead pets. First it was a nice yellow Labrador. He was OK apparently, keeping her mother company. Then there was a squirrel. Yes, she was glad to hear the squirrel was all right as well. And then there was a tortoise. Will and I had to stop ourselves laughing out loud. 'God,' I said, 'please don't let me be communicated with by a tortoise.'

The next time we went things were a bit more interesting. The medium was a Scottish woman and she picked me out. She said there was a woman in a red sari holding a crystal and saying she thought I was going to do something special with my life. I was thinking this might be my 'ayah' and was very pleased she remembered me. And then, the medium said, there was a woman with blue eyes who loved horses. That had to be my mother if it was anyone. She said the money I had inherited was mine to do what I liked with. How did she know about that? I accepted the message and was quite impressed. At least there were no tortoises involved.

Will and I went once more. This time we arrived rather late and had to sit in the front row. The medium came to us almost immediately. He spoke to Will first, said he had his father with him and how pleased he was to say 'hello' and tell him what a splendid boy he was. He said he was the sort of person who would give anything away to someone who said they needed it. And that was fine. That was the way he was. All very satisfactory! He then turned to me and said I had had a rough period, but it was time I got out into the world and did what I had come here for. I thought then, *What I really want to do was to continue exploring my past lives,* but I had no idea where to start.

I went home and looked through the pages of a copy of *Kindred Spirit* which someone had given me. I ringed the name of one person who sounded likely but still did nothing about it. Then one evening Will wanted to watch a programme about Gerald Scarfe in which the cartoonist was exploring attitudes to death and the afterlife. Halfway through there was a woman called Diane Park who was doing past lifework. She was a middle-aged Australian woman, very down to earth and funny and I knew I'd found my teacher. I took down her name and decided I would ring the BBC the next day to find out how to get hold of her. Then I went back to the magazine and found it was her name I had ringed.

I phoned Diane the next day. She said she was about to start her last London training and still had places, did I want to come? Yes. That was the next weekend so I had to organise for someone to look after Will who was about eleven at the time. I rang some good friends in Eye who said, yes, he could stay with them but they were going off to Dance Camp – a yearly assembly of people camped in a field in Norfolk where they danced, played music and generally explored alternative ways of being. So I went off to for my introductory weekend and he went to Dance Camp where he learned to drum and came back a dedicated musician with a desire for a djembe.

I had no idea what to expect. I wondered if my fellow students would all be a bit flaky – hippies even. What I found was two lawyers, an actress, a nurse, someone who had worked for the Min. of Ag. and was now a yoga teacher and one therapist. I introduced myself as a playwright.

After a brief introduction Diane sent us straight into a session. We worked in pairs and were given a script which involved helping your partner meet their spirit guide. When my turn came I found myself at the bottom of a flight of steps waiting for someone to turn up. My first sensation was of my right eyelid twitching, as though someone were trying to get my attention. I mentioned this to my partner. Ask who it is, she said. So I did. What I then saw was a word written in caps in tiny type just at the edge of my field of vision. GOD. I laughed out loud. God and I, if he/she exists, have always had a difficult relationship and whoever it was obviously didn't want to alarm me.

I saw this hooded figure standing further up the steps. This apparently was my guide but I couldn't see his face. I asked him a couple of questions and he gave me some answers which seemed to fit. I then asked to see his face and, of course, it was William. Again I laughed and asked him why he didn't show himself immediately? He said, 'I knew you wouldn't take my answers seriously if you knew who I was.'

My first past life session was scheduled for the next training weekend and days beforehand I knew what it was about. For years I'd been haunted by the First World War. I had an uncle who had lost a leg at the Somme and when I first saw *Oh! What a Lovely War* I was transfixed by the statistics. Days before I was due to go to London I could feel my body getting ready. Most marked of all was a tightness in my shoulders which wouldn't go away.

We were all finding our way at this stage and I was paired up with tough a little Scottish woman who would normally take no prisoners. She took me through the induction into the past life. Where was I? I was outside. In the country. I was breathless. I had been running. She asked me to look down at my body and see what I was wearing? I was wearing khaki trousers and heavy boots. On my top nothing but a vest. What was my name? 'Tom'. I was a man in his thirties and I was running from the battlefield. I wasn't running because I was scared. I was running from the horror of it all. My best friend – called Percy – had been blown up in front of me and died in my arms. I was running to get away.

Suddenly there is someone else there. A young officer, bright and clean and polished. He clearly hasn't been to the front. He has a pistol in his hand. He wants to know what I am doing there? I am full of rage. I tell him what I think of the war. Of the young men, the boys, who are dying in the trenches, and for what? He wants me to go back to my company. I laugh in his face. Sneer at his patriotism and his naivety. He accuses me of cowardice. That is the last straw. I move towards him. He probably thinks I'm going to kill him. He shoots. I see the bullet coming towards me. I feel the impact but no pain. I die instantly.

Now I am being told to heal the body. I stand over it as the spirit of Tom and look at myself. He has a nice, craggy face. A kind face. He has already been wounded once. There is a scar on his forehead. I feel quite emotional. My partner tells me to remove the bullet which killed me. The bullet is clean and bright. I laugh, thinking about this young man and how his Batman keeps everything clean and tidy

132

for him, puts a handkerchief in his pocket like his mother might. I feel both contemptuous and fatherly.

We look for the emotions buried in the body in the form of objects or shadows or live creatures that have become trapped. We look for my anger. I was very angry. I find it in my shoulders. I take it out. It is smooth and hard, like polished granite and I don't want to get rid of it.

Suddenly Diane is above me. 'Do you always like the shape of your anger?' she asks and I realise I do. I like to be right. Anger is how I have defined my whole life. With my father. With my brother. Ex-lovers. Anyone I think has let me down. Probably with myself. I get rid of the piece of stone. Lots of other things are taken away and I go and visit the wife and son I will leave behind. I hope they won't think I was shot as a coward.

This was an extraordinary life to heal. I began to realise that I had been walking about in a state of shock. Whether it was personal to me or my family or the world it didn't matter. Somewhere, at some level, I felt I had shifted something very important.

Later I wrote a radio play, *Always the Guns*, in which the officer goes to the front and is buried in the mud and unable to hear. The ghost of Tom talks him through the night, tells him when to call for the stretcher party, probably saves his life. In the play I called him Robert.

---

*So here I am locked up with a lot of other mad people. 'At least it won't be noticed in me here, for here the men are as mad as me.' Not that I feel mad. Don't think most of them are either. I have a very nice doctor who just comes and talks to me and I talk to the other inmates, although mostly they can't understand a word I say. There's an old man who sits by a pool in the garden. I talk to him. He doesn't move. Just sits. Once he looked up and seemed to see me. I could see myself reflected in his eyes. I looked like two angels dressed in white. But someone told me he is blind. What does it matter? I see myself when he looks at me.*

*Tell Mum I'm alright and I am praying for her and for you and everyone. A palmist in Amritsar said I'd return to England for a spell this year... so who knows...?*
*Your sister in Allah,*
*Saarah xxxx*

---

# JUDGEMENT

*ROBERT: His was the last voice I heard. That voice in my head. The voice of the soldier that I shot because he stood between me and glory. Between me and what I thought was right. What I had been brought up to think was right.*

*I didn't think he was on my side that day. Demolishing every patriotic illusion I was armed with. I didn't want to shoot him. I wanted him to go away and leave me alone. He scared the living daylights out of me with his words and his anger and his sheer bloody-mindedness. I thought he was going to kill me.*

*My legs mended soon enough but my ears didn't. They sent me home. No use once I couldn't hear an order. I came home and my mother was thankful. And I never told anyone that the first person, possibly the only person I killed, was a man from my own side.*

*ALWAYS THE GUNS*

I was only halfway through the Past Life training when the possibility of doing a Soul Retrieval workshop came up. It was explained to me that we sometimes lose part of our soul energy through emotional trauma, accident or illness. Usually we recover quite naturally but sometimes these fragmented parts stay missing. We've all heard of people say things like, 'Part of me left when she died,' and post-traumatic stress disorder often leaves people trapped in the memories that have caused the condition. We may live our whole lives in response to these missing parts, as though we are in mourning for what we have lost. Soul retrieval is a process which enables you to bring these fragments back and reintegrate them.

I liked the idea of this and thought Lucia probably had

135

a great deal missing, what with her lost childhood and, more recently, the road accident. So I suggested she came too.

We met halfway at a rather old-fashioned hotel in Windsor, which brought back memories for both of us of childhood teas with our grandmothers. Cucumber sandwiches. Scones with cream. Proper tea. China cups and tea strainers. I left my car in the car park and we drove on in Lucia's new car to Cornwall. I can't remember what it was but it was low and fast. Lucia liked her cars.

We arrived at a Napoleonic fort built on the edge of a cliff. The walls were ten feet thick, a feature that became very important as the workshop proceeded. It was a big group and several of them were practised in emotional release on a big scale.

One evening, when there had been a considerable amount of weeping and wailing, Lucia took me aside and said, 'I'm not coming on holiday with you again. I don't think you can have read the brochure properly.' We laughed ourselves silly. Acknowledging our emotions, once we'd recognised them, had never been a problem for either of us. But we were still children of the Empire and there was no need to go overboard.

The first session was to make contact with a power animal, or spirit helper, so they could accompany us on our journey to find our lost soul fragments. We were instructed to find a river and a guide to accompany us. We would know we had found our power animal when we had seen it three times.

My guide is an African in a dugout canoe. I have a picture of just such a man from a year I spent doing VSO in Sierra Leone. We step into the boat and he moves out onto the river. The place is teaming with wildlife but I am almost immediately aware of an elephant moving along the bank beside us. I like elephants so much that I delay choosing it

136

in case I am simply fulfilling a wish. I see some vultures. I see the vultures twice. The elephant is still there. The vultures seem to be saying, 'If you don't get on and choose the elephant you'll get us.' So I go with my wish and acknowledge the elephant. Not that I entirely dismiss the vultures since they are very useful in clearing away unwanted remains and I knew there are still plenty of rotting corpses littering my inner landscape.

In Lucia's session we had trouble finding the guide. She arrived at a jetty as instructed. And there was someone there. But she didn't seem to think he was her guide.

'Ask him his name,' I say.

'Wazier, that's what he says. What sort of name is that?'

'Are you sure he isn't saying vizier. Isn't that some kind of eastern court official?' I ask.

'Suppose he could be but what's he doing here?'

'And you don't think he's the guide?'

'No, he says he's not my guide. But he keeps saying "Wazier" and don't know why?'

'Ask him.'

'He just looks at me and says "Wazier" again.' Then she starts laughing.

'What's so funny?'

'Wazier. That's not his name. He saying my guide "was here" but he's gone.'

We both laugh. 'Will he take you on the bloody river anyway?' I ask.

'Oh yes, he doesn't mind taking me on the river, but he wants me to know he's not my guide and he won't be turning up again.'

We do the journey. Collect her power animal – can't remember what it was – and come back equipped for the first soul retrieval session.

In my soul retrieval session my guide, as ever, is

William – not the African who had come to take me down the river. William's not much help. He seems to sit around waiting for me to get on with it but he keeps me amused. He finds me a place on a hill to work from and we go in search of the part of me that is missing. The elephant comes with us.

It takes me a little while to find the soul fragment. When I see her she is up a tree, the apple tree I used to play in when I was a child. It was at the end of the orchard with branches reaching out over the hedge, so that I could sit perched above the cornfield like a sailor at the prow of his ship. The corn moving in the wind like water. I loved this place. I came here to dream, to have adventures, to escape. Whenever anyone upset me I would go up my tree and forget them. They couldn't hurt me there. They couldn't even reach me. And there I was, aged about six, defiantly sitting up my tree, still there after more than forty years.

I am my adult self, standing under the old apple tree, trying to persuade my little girl self to come with me. The child looks at me. Doesn't seem to want to know. I climb the tree, tell her who I am and that I've come to collect her. She glares at me and says she's not going anywhere with me. I'm an old fart and she's sure I wear twinsets, have my hair permed and go to coffee mornings. I suggest she looks again. I am wearing jeans and a bright pink ethnic sweater with elephants all over it and I've climbed this tree. Is this old fart behaviour? She seems to be considering this, but still doesn't seem to be very interested in coming with me.

Then she sees the elephant. It is just the right height for her to climb onto its back from the branch. And we're off. She wants to ride it all round the village, show everyone that she has an elephant to ride on. Then she wants to ride it to India. My partner (not Lucia) says, 'Hang on a minute, we are supposed to be finding out why she went up the tree in the first place.'

At this point I become the little girl. She has been up her tree all afternoon and it is teatime. Daddy has spread a blanket in the orchard, Mummy has brought the tea out and Charlotte is there. We're going to have a picnic. I come down to join in, but nobody seems interested in my arrival or what I have to say, so I go back up the tree and sulk. They finish the tea and go in. I stay up the tree. It's getting dark. My father comes and says it's time for bed. I say I don't care, I'm not coming. He just shrugs and walks off. I am furious.

My partner suggests I get my little girl to talk to him. We follow him indoors. He's sitting in the drawing room where the tiger rug is. He is reading the paper. The child says she's cross with him. He says, 'Oh yes,' and goes on reading. She is thinking, *If I could shoot a tiger, then he'd notice me.* But there aren't any tigers to shoot. She thinks, *If I shot him, then he'd see I meant business.* But when she imagines the scene he just wanders off into the kitchen saying to my mother, 'That bloody child, she's just shot me.' That wouldn't work either. I am furious with him.

My partner suggests the little girl asks him why he didn't play with her, if that's what she wanted? This time he looks up and says, 'I haven't got my little boy either. I left him behind in India when they sent me home to school. The little boy who would have played with you has gone.'

Now there's no stopping her, this little girl of mine, she is going to go to India and find the little boy for her Daddy and that's that. My partner does his best to try and keep things under control, but she says she's not going anywhere with me until this is done.

We are in India. We seem to be on top of a mountain sitting round a campfire under the stars. I am there with my

139

father as a young man, and both children. There is an old man, who took my father pig-sticking when he was over a hundred, the old man not my father. His name is Makhdoum, which causes my partner some amusement as he thinks it sounds like Private Frazer of 'We're doomed, Mr Mainwaring!' from *Dad's Army*.

Then of course there is William. I introduce him to my father which he finds a little difficult. He is after all the man who gave him a grandson and then buggered off, not the story you'd expect as an officer and a gentleman. They shake hands rather formally, but I think my father is secretly rather amused by the whole thing. Makhdoum is making something wonderful on the fire for us to eat and my father and I sit together as we never did as adults whilst the children play. It is a magical moment.

My partner suggests that it is time I asked my little girl if she will come back into me to be part of me again? She's not too sure about this, but Makhdoum says, 'I'll show you, little memsahib. I'll show you how. I'll put the Sahib's little boy back in and then you will know how it is done.' He picks up my father's little boy and makes him grow very small, so he can hold him in the palm of his hand. Then he puts him into my father through his heart.

The little girl is wild with excitement, she thinks this is magic and wants him to do it for her. Makhdoum says, 'No, I am the person who must do this for her, because I am her.'

At this point the child turns and looks at me with new interest. 'You can do magic?' she says. 'You are a magician too?'

I say. 'But, of course, how else do you think I was able to come and find you?'

She wants to know if I will go on doing magic when she comes back in and I say yes. She wants me to promise we will have adventures and climb trees. All of which I am glad to agree to, since my whole life is an adventure. So at last she is happy to come back to me.

My father and I say goodbye and he goes off with Makhdoum. I think as he goes, *Doing a soul retrieval for your father must beat tiger shooting any day. Anyone with a gun can shoot a tiger. It takes someone very special to make this journey.*

I think of that determined little girl who refused to do anything we asked until we had done what she wanted and realised this was the quality I had been missing all those years. I am so excited to have her back. I am also quite frightened. I go about for days afraid that she will go away again. It is like finding a child you didn't know you'd lost and being horrified at being so neglectful.

All the way home in the car my elephant follows me. There are zoo signs which appear several times with an elephant as emblem. Then the little girl makes her presence known. On the evening we get back someone gives us two tickets for a Paul Merton show. I am very tired but I know Will really wants to go, so I buy another ticket and we head off. Lucia and Will sit together, I take the single seat. I keep going to sleep, but wake up for one very important moment in the show. Paul Merton is doing a sketch which involves a performance by invisible poodles. The star turn is called Pepe and at some stage in the sketch Pepe disappears and everyone in the audience is exhorted to shout, 'Pepe come home…!' I hear them calling, calling to the little girl in me. As I open my eyes the invisible Pepe returns, riding on an old-fashioned child's tricycle of the kind I used to have when I was small.

The next day Lucia and I are walking down the main street in Woodbridge and there is a little girl being really stroppy with her daddy, refusing to do whatever he wants her to do. The entire range of her vocabulary seems to be,

'No.' I turn to Lucia and say, 'That's me. That's what I've got back. That marvellous refusal to do anything I don't want.' The man says, clear as a bell, 'Peppy. Come on now…' Believe me, I am telling it just how it was…

Of course we did work on Lucia's child as well, or someone else did. She found a wonderful old guide, not unlike mine, a man called Wunjo – the name of a rune stone that means peace. She travelled through steaming jungles to find her child, who was still with the medicine man who had given her her name in Nigeria, at least that's how I remember it now. I think she also did some work on whatever part of herself travelled in the realms beyond after the accident. What she remembered was she would never have come back if she hadn't heard her son calling her home.

These were strange days, full of all kinds of esoteric experiences. I went on to train other past life healers and Lucia came to my workshops, both as someone to practice on and as a practitioner. She got some very interesting clients. One woman gave her a set of dining room furniture, a table and six very ornate chairs. Lucia remarked casually that they looked as though they had come out of Versailles. Later she did a session with the woman, only to discover she was indeed an inhabitant of the Sun King's palace, possibly Marie Antoinette.

Here I think I need to dispel the myth that people who experience past lives always turn out to be someone famous. Usually they are somebody very ordinary, someone who had real disappointments in their lives which they need to clear. But occasionally you come across someone of great significance. During my training I came across two Virgin Marys and decided the people were involved with some kind of work on the collective consciousness of what it was to be a mother and shadowed

142

by a mythological figure. Indeed does it matter whether the experience is a direct personal memory or a way of creating a scenario which allows you to deal with a trauma in this life, the effect is the same.

Sometimes I also felt we might be clearing shared cultural or ancestral memories. We are all affected by history and the stories we have been told. And that also has significance.

---

*'What did you do after you got the letter?' Persey asks me.*

*'I rang the Foreign Office of course, what else? And they communicated with the British Consul. He went round to see her. She just said she'd didn't want to go home. She was happy there. England was a colonial wasteland. He said he thought she was being looked after. Then I got a phone call from the Foreign Office. The Consul had called. He thought they wanted to have her committed and it would cost money. He wanted her out of there. He put her on a plane. Sent her home. Think mother met her at the airport.*

*'And then what?'*

*'Nothing really. Mum always used to act on the assumption – with animals as well as people – that if you kept them warm and safe they would get better. But Charlotte seemed to stay in bed all day. She knew there was something wrong, but she didn't know what to do.'*

*'How dreadful. How could she survive that?'*

*'I don't know. I never asked. We just lived through it. But I did think when she had her stroke perhaps part of her had gone to Charlotte so she could look after all her children.'*

*'Dreadful.'*

---

# THE WORLD

*ROBERT: Without him I would probably have drowned in the mud. Died of cold and terror. Without him my sons would never have been born. My grandchildren would not run in the garden or climb the trees to laugh at their silly old granddad who can't see what they are saying from so far up in the branches. Without him...*
*ALWAYS THE GUNS*

Lucia was off again. This time to Rhodes where she met a man who wanted to rent her a hotel. She and the boys worked all through the winter and got a contract with one of the tour companies. All seemed to be going well and I heard from her occasionally. Then, after a gap of some months, I got another of those phone calls.

Lucia spoke. 'Hello, it's me.'

I recognised her voice. 'Hello, how are you?' I ask in a purely conversational way.

'Not very well actually.'

'Not another bloody accident, I hope?'

'I went to see the doctor. He told me to go home.'

'What? What's wrong?'

'I've got a flight booked for tomorrow evening. Arriving in Stansted. Don't suppose you could collect me?'

'Is it serious?'

'Think so. Can you?'

'Course I can. What time?'

I stood in the almost deserted arrival hall at Stansted at one o'clock in the morning and watched this little figure emerging through the arrival doors. At first she didn't seem to see me. She just stood there, dressed in a short skirt and her usual stacked heels, neat as a pin and blown up like a barrel. This wasn't anything trivial.

We go straight to the car. We are driving.

'What did they say it was?' I ask.

'Not sure till they've looked at me. The doctor said I couldn't afford treatment in Greece. I must go home immediately. I tried to argue with him. Said I had a hotel to run. Couldn't we wait till the end of the season. He took my hand and looked into my eyes and said, 'You don't have time to wait. Go now.' That's what I like about the Greeks they tell it how it is. Think he said it might be ovarian cancer.'

'Oh shit.'

'Precisely.'

'Still we don't know yet. Let's get home first.'

We arrived in Woodbridge in the early hours. Neither of us knowing what was ahead of us.

First thing in the morning I got her to the surgery where a very nice woman doctor, a locum, took one look at her bloated body and booked her in with a specialist in the hospital that afternoon.

We waited in a corridor for her name to be called and then, there we were, with the surgeon. No messing around here. They admitted her immediately and set about draining the fluid. The next step was going to be a hysterectomy. Soon as possible. There must have been blood tests and there were endless people asking her questions and filling in forms. The one thing she repeatedly pointed out was that she was allergic to penicillin.

Luckily for us she was given a private room and I could stay with her most of the time. Much as I admire and support our National Health Service, you need a minder if anything complicated is happening. Just as she was about to be wheeled off for the operation the anaesthetist appeared and asked, once again, whether she allergic to anything. I almost shouted 'PENICILLIN' at him.

On the plus side the nurses assured us we were getting the best surgeon in the hospital and I believed them. She was a lovely, straightforward woman and she did a great job. Lucia was sitting up in bed and playing silly games with me in almost no time.

But our problems weren't over. Because Lucia had changed both her names and sounded distinctly foreign I came in one morning to find the Bursar had been in to complain about her coming into the country to sponge off the NHS. I was furious and told him so. She was as English as I was and he had no business berating her in the state she was in.

There was also a problem when she dressed up to go to the café. Short skirt. High heels. You could see that some of the women thought she was looking far too glamorous for someone in need of urgent medical attention. I wouldn't have bothered. I'd have shuffled down the corridor in my slippers, but not Lucia.

There were, of course, all sorts of blood tests to see if the cancer had been cleared and we were told we would be called for an appointment. We went home and hadn't heard anything after about a week. Her surgeon was on holiday. We went to see the GP who felt we shouldn't have to wait any longer and made us an appointment at the hospital clinic.

Sitting in the waiting room Lucia got the giggles. 'Will you look at them in their dolly wigs. I'm not wearing a dolly wig whatever they say.'

Her name was called. We went in, to be confronted by a very flustered Chinese doctor who was clearly very annoyed that he had been given the job of telling her anything. 'This is not my job,' he kept saying, 'I shouldn't have to be doing this. I have told them in the office, this is not my job.'

'Well. Whether it is your job or not, could you tell us the results of the tests?' I say.

He looked at the papers for some time and then gave us a short lecture on the different degrees of cancer that might be indicated by the results. If it was first degree, that was good apparently, but as we went up the scale the prognosis didn't sound very encouraging. When you got to four it sounded as though it was just a matter of time. He clearly didn't want to tell us anything which made us both rather nervous.

'So,' says Lucia, smiling sweetly, 'what degree are you going to award me?'

The poor man didn't find this very funny. In fact he didn't find it funny at all. I'm not sure he even knew the answer. We came away completely confused as to how good her chances were. His view seemed to be that she would be well-advised to move on to chemotherapy and said the oncologist would be able to advise us better.

'You think I'm a deader?' she asks as we drive home.

'Don't know. We'll have to see how it goes. Are you going to have chemo?'

'Have to see what the oncologist says, I suppose. Will you help me shave off my hair?'

'If we get that far.'

We drive in silence for a while. 'You think we shouldn't do that? The chemo?' she asks.

'I think we should do everything.'

'But we know how to clear this, don't we? Isn't that what all the work has been about, being able to heal ourselves?' she says.

'We'll try everything of course, but no amount of past lives would have drained that fluid,' I say.

And then we got the appointment that mattered. The one with the oncologist. 'Ah,' he says, looking up to see this glamorous little figure standing in his consulting room. 'Now you look young and strong, we can give you the works.'

They liked each other from the start. This was a good sign. But she kept saying she wanted to get back to her boys and the hotel in Greece which made me nervous. I had no idea what effect taking her on was having on my GP's surgery finances and there was the ever-vigilant Bursar.

The oncologist gave her to understand they had taken out the major site of the cancer but no one could be sure that everything had been cleared so chemotherapy was highly recommended. 'We want to give you the best chance,' he says. 'You sound as though you have things to do.'

We dithered for a bit. We did a few sessions and asked her guides what was necessary, but decided in the end we should take his advice, yet approach it in our own way.

First thing was to make friends with the drug they would be using. The oncologist said that Taxol was the best poison for ovarian cancer, product of the European yew tree. We liked the idea that it was a natural product, however poisonous, and decided to treat it with due respect.

So first thing we did was to drive out to a local churchyard and address the spirit of the yew trees. We left small offerings and came home with leaves and berries to ensure that the spirit of the trees stayed with us. This particular graveyard contained some of my rediscovered ancestors which added significance for us.

Yew trees properly addressed, we proceeded to the first appointment for the chemo. Lucia was still not really sure whether she wanted to go through with this. She sat with the nurse, who was finding it difficult to locate a vein, and asked her what she thought, did she think the chemo would do any good?

The nurse looked up at the bag of solution suspended above her and said, 'There is about five thousand pounds worth of the drug in that bag. We don't spend that kind of money if we think it won't do any good.'

To begin with I used to go and sit with her while she had her chemo, but later she went on her own and came back with all sorts of stories. Her hair did start to fall out and I shaved it off for her. And she did get a dolly wig but she didn't wear it more than once. Instead we went to a wig shop and bought two splendid specimens which gave her a choice between a blond bob and a cap of dark straight hair, neither of which looked in the least bit artificial.

Apart from a couple of days just after the chemo, she seemed to feel quite all right. She said she forgot all about the cancer most of the time and just got on with things, one of these being to go and visit her daughter and grandchildren in London. The rest of the time she stayed with me.

We went to homoeopaths, acupuncturists, clairvoyants, healers of all kinds and descriptions. She drank strange potions, water distilled from remote lakes, herbal infusions handed down by shamans, a kind of yoghurt originating in the Himalayas. We left no stone unturned. We even visited a psychic surgeon who rummaged around on her stomach and seemed to throw something hard into a wastepaper basket. Quite often we had to stop ourselves from getting the giggles.

And of course we continued to explore her past lives and went looking for soul fragments. We had collected her two-year-old self in Cornwall, but there was a child of seven and a teenager and plenty of soul energy left with her various lovers. She also went to meet the man who gave her her African name. I thought if anyone knew what to do it would be him.

When we weren't doing these esoteric things we went for walks in the woods, spent hours by the river, went dancing, watched daytime TV and just talked – about life and death and the possibility of an afterlife and what she might want to order for her next life?

She said once, 'I must have done something good in a previous life to have a friend to walk with me through this.' I didn't always feel like a good friend.

At one point she wanted to go to Lourdes. I wasn't too keen, mainly because I didn't want to travel so far. I still had a tendency to want to hold to the territory I had marked out for myself. Instead I persuaded her that we had our own pilgrimage site at Walsingham in North Norfolk. Here we wandered around finding ways of connecting with the place. We attended small services, both Catholic and C of E, and went on part of a pilgrim walk through the town, although by this point I think we were both getting tired and rather bored. I think the highlight was finding the stone which marked the position of the original chapel and both of us kneeling to kiss it. Lucia looked and me and said, 'Did you ever, in your wildest dreams, imagine we would end up doing something like this?' And we laughed and hoped and went and bought a couple of souvenirs. I think I still have mine somewhere.

There was one particular incident that kept us amused for a day or two. We were sitting on a grassy bank by an isolated stretch of river. A wonderful empty landscape which can't have changed in centuries. Some birds. An old fishing boat. A dinghy tied to a jetty.

A man appeared on the bank above us and asked if we wanted to cross the river. He was the ferryman. Thinking of the ferryman on the River Styx who took dead souls to the other side, I didn't think crossing a river with a ferryman was a good omen at this stage. So, I asked if he would take us for a row on the river instead, which he obligingly did. I said we didn't want to get to the other side, not yet anyway. I didn't explain.

We were rowing up and down the river and I spotted a boot upturned on a post beside the jetty on the other side. 'What's that doing there,' I ask him, 'that boot on the pole?'

'Oh,' he says. 'That's John's boot.'

'John?'

'Long story.'

'We're not in any hurry,' says Lucia.

He adjusts his oars to take us out into the stream.

'Well,' he says, 'when I first came down here from London I got a little boat. Used to row over to that side of the river. Wandered about a bit. And then one day I was just pulling it ashore when this woman rode up on a horse. What did I think I was doing? she said. I said, I was thinking of going for a walk. This was private land, she said. I obviously wasn't from around here. No, I said, indeed I was not. I was a London lad and I thought you could go anywhere in the countryside as long as you shut the gates and didn't do any harm. Not any more, she said, not round here and watched me get into the boat and row off.

'Now, I'm not a belligerent sort of bloke but I wasn't going to have this. I went off and did a bit of research and found there used to be a ferry here before the First World War and that if I re-established it all the footpaths on that side of the river would come back into use. Well, now, who could resist a challenge like that? So I set to. Began building a new jetty on this side of the river.'

'And John?' I ask.

151

'Hang on a minute, I'm telling you a story.'

At this point Lucia spots a Godwit. They are biggish birds and she liked the name. Bit like a halfwit with a touch of the omnipotent. Perhaps this was *The Fool* returning for the final run.

The ferryman continued, 'I was cutting the hedge back home, up a ladder, and I heard this voice speaking to me from the other side. 'You the man who's mending the ferry?' I climbed a bit further up the ladder to see this bloke standing in the road. Big bloke. Dressed in work clothes and a cloth cap. Bit pasty for a countryman but he looked strong enough.'

'Who's asking?' I say.

'I'm your next-door neighbour. 'Cottage on that side. You want a hand?'

'Was he any good?' Lucia asks.

'Bloody marvellous. Down here every day. Digging like a man looking for gold. Said he used to row over on a Sunday to go and see his granny in the big house. She was the cook. Probably fed the family on the sly.'

'Been here all his life then?'

'Born in the cottage, stayed in the cottage. Don't think he'd ever gone much further than Woodbridge. Some chap in the pub said he'd been engaged and the girl had died in the house and he didn't tell anybody for weeks. No one had seen him for ages.'

'Came to help you though.'

'Thinking of his old gran and her posh dinners, I expect.'

'When do we get to the boot?' asks Lucia, who I think was getting rather bored or just wanted a bit of peace and quiet. It was the most glorious day and I suppose we should have been concentrating on the scenery.

'Yes well... it was one of those scorching days. Sun

splitting the stones. We had been working for a while and John stopped and said he didn't feel too good. We'd nearly finished this side and I was keen to get on so I said, 'Come on, John, twenty minutes more and we'll be done. I'll take you up to the pub for a couple of pints to celebrate.' He turned back to his spade and I turned away to do whatever I was doing. Then I heard a thud. I looked round and there he was, laid out like a beached whale, dead as a door nail.'

'I thought we were trying to avoid death,' says Lucia, looking hard at me with those black button eyes.

'No, let him finish,' I say.' We still haven't got to the boot.'

'Yes, the boot. Well, it was sometime later. I was battling on on my own. Raining this time. Pouring. I'd come out in my trainers of all things and I remembered John had a pair of boots he left under the quay for days like this. So I go looking for them. One was OK, full of water but serviceable. Other one, some animal had been nesting in it, chewed a hole in the toe. No good to anyone. I kept the good one. Put it on the pole when I finished. Sort of tribute to John.'

'And that's it?'

'Thought he'd like it. What do you think?'

'Hope nobody's going to put any boots up for me,' says Lucia.

'What's she on about?' asks the ferryman.

'Bit of a cancer scare. But she's not dead yet,' I say.

'Sorry to hear that. Sorry to have bored you with my story.'

'Oh, I wasn't bored,' I say. 'But can we go back now?'

He took us back to the bank and we wandered off along the path back to the car.

'Was that a good omen or not do you think?' Lucia asks as we walk away.

153

## A last phone call

'Char?'

'Yes.'

'How are you?'

'Waiting.'

'For what?'

'For death.'

'Well, while you're waiting, why don't you come over and see us?'

'What for?'

'I've a play I'm putting on. You'd enjoy that. And you could come help me type up my book. And John's got an election. There's plenty to do.'

'For God's sake. I can hardly get out of bed. Let alone sit in front of a typewriter.'

'Oh, come on. You'd be alright if you had something to do. We got by last time. And it won't be for long.'

'I don't want to be involved in all that trivia. I just want to die. Why won't anyone understand that? I want to fucking die.'

'We've heard it all so often.'

'This time it's what I want. This time there's nothing else.'

'Then get on with it or shut up about it. Don't you know what you do to mother with all these endless dramas?'

'Me? What about you? Writing to her saying you're leaving and that you're having an affair.'

'That was over months ago. That was the point.'

'Oh, I thought you were. Anyway I'm not bloody coming to do your manual labour. Hold the place together until you deign to leave.'

'Be like that. I don't care. I'm not sure I want to come home though. Not if you're around.'

'Well, fuck you.'

# THE FOOL

*ISOBEL: I can go back into the garden. Walk the boxed paths to the old wall where there are figs and peaches. Watch Alf moving like a fish among the asparagus ferns. Lie in the nursery at night and listen to the rain bubbling in the gutters. I was frightened of water then. I could feel it rising. Lapping softly in the leaves around my window. One night when I was ill, I had a temperature, I woke to feel my bed floating. Moving in the water. And I screamed and screamed and no one came. I died that night. I will die again and the water will carry me away... nice water, blue water, baby in the water...*

*MOTHERING SUNDAY*

It is September. The night is warm. There is are clouds. Deep soft clouds like bedding. A full moon occasionally emerges to draw the house and garden into the quiet light of a distant sun. An owl calls.

A group of us are sitting round a brazier. There are flares planted in the lawn. In the background there is an old farmhouse. The lights occasionally reflected in a window. Between us and the house there is pile of hay that shifts and breathes and occasionally coughs.

I am sitting with a group of friends. Holding a vigil. The pile of hay contains Lucia. We are trying to cheat death.

The idea came to me one night sitting by her bed in the hospital. I decided to consult one of my spirit guides. What could I do? The guide who appeared was an African medicine man. Could have been the medicine man who gave her her name.

We were in an African village. Huts. A clearing. No one else there but him and me. He was showing me a depression in the ground, a kind of shallow grave, which was covered with bark. 'You can sometimes cheat death,' he said, 'if you make him think he already has his prey.'

I was up for anything. So was Lucia. So we invented a ritual. We would go to the house in the country where I did past life training and enact her funeral. Make death think she was already dead.

I assembled my Past Life practitioners and asked if they would join me. No problem there. Two of us set out to find the local organic farmer who supplied us with two bales of hay and was very interested in what we were going to use it for.

Back at the house we set up the site. We were going to bury Lucia in the hay and keep watch all night. Hence the brazier and flares. First, we decided we would take the opportunity to assess all of our lives. What if we were about to meet Death? What would we say for ourselves? What would death have to say to us?

I had a wonderful black cloak, an Irish wedding cloak that had been given to me by Adam's father. A cloak and a death mask. We took turns. I don't think I was very good at playing death but Lucia was spine-tingling and very honest. She knew me far too well. Mainly she thanked me for walking with her through this ordeal and helping her to face death in whatever form it came. You will note that I cannot seem to avoid the subject, feel as though I have been patrolling that border for a very long time.

I remembered the first thing I wrote when I arrived on my hill in Kent. I was walking one day in this beautiful countryside and I had a vision of Death walking beside me. My sense was that this was the ultimate lover. He knew you when you were born. He watched you grow. And as you grew older he stole you for himself, so that in the end only *he* could see how beautiful you were. By the same token I have always hoped that for men Death appears as a woman. She does in the Celtic tradition.

When we felt the time was right we put Lucia to bed in her cradle of hay and walked round her calling her African name into the night, hoping the medicine man who welcomed her into the world would help us hide her from her pursuer. Then we all settled down to keep watch.

I had expected it to be a very long cold night and that I would want to go to sleep. As it was none of us blinked. Something about the unexpected warmth, the moonlight, the company and the task kept us awake. Lucia slept. We sat and chatted. The various sounds that issued from the pile of hay kept us amused. We weren't at all sure that the farmer hadn't turned up to see what we were doing, as at one point we thought we could hear voices in the field on the other side of the hedge. Perhaps he expected us to be dancing naked round the fire. If so he went away disappointed.

Lucia survived the first round of chemo very well and went back to Greece to run the hotel with her sons. She even set up a workshop for the past life practitioners and another group of women who were into psychic healing. I don't think I behaved very well, as I didn't think you got much done on the healing front if you weren't prepared to dig deep into your own process. Still we did some interesting exercises and it was wonderful to be in Greece again.

We travelled round the island quite a bit and there was one place we came to where there was a tunnel built to carry water from a stream into a lake. It was about six-foot high and only wide enough for one person at a time. I wanted to go through it but was never very keen on enclosed spaces and certainly didn't want to go down it with a crowd of people. No one else wanted to go with me anyway. I didn't really want to go on my own and wished for a young man

157

to escort me. At that moment a Dutch man turned up and agreed to lead me through. Another of those strange journeys to the underworld which I survived. Lucia wasn't with us or I am sure she would not have hesitated.

We left her at the hotel in Greece looking quite her old self and busy shocking the customers by wandering about rather scantily clad and telling them what they could and couldn't do in her establishment in no uncertain terms. She had also grown a tight cap of black curls which was quite unlike the wavy hair she'd had before.

Everything went very well for another year and then I got another phone call. It was spring. She was in and out of hospital in Rhodes and wanted me there to help the boys get the hotel ready for the season. A very good friend went with me.

I said to her, 'I have to go and look after Lucia.'

She said, 'But who's going to look after you?' So she came too.

We didn't stay in the hotel this time but in a magical courtyard that had once been the residence of some local monks. I loved it. Don't think my friend did. She felt the presence of an unquiet spirit. A monk who she thought might have committed suicide. But I woke each morning to the sun in the courtyard and a breakfast of fresh bread and yoghurt, which I bought, speaking in my best Greek, from the shop next door.

One morning during breakfast in the courtyard there was an earth tremor. A strange sensation in which the world in which we depended on to be solid and reliable could be nothing of the sort. A sort of dislocation. I think it was a Sunday as the church bell began to toll shortly after.

Back at the hotel we did a lot of scrubbing and washing pans but we also went to the beach and I got to swim in the sea.

Things got a bit worse and Lucia was taken into hospital again. We went down to be with her and were not at all sure it was a safe place to be. The doctor wandered around in a bloodstained coat and there were no nurses to speak of, or to. The woman in the next bed was clearly being looked after by her daughter. I came to the conclusion that you needed a minder to feed, wash and water you.

We left because we had booked the plane, but not long after Lucia was back in hospital in Ipswich where she and the oncologist came to the mutual conclusion that there was not much point in subjecting her to another round of chemo.

I have to say that the last few weeks in which she was in hospital were an inspiration. Every morning she woke and embarked on various projects to keep herself occupied. She embroidered a cushion cover for her eldest son and spent quite a lot of time planning her next life. She had told her youngest son, Oliver, she would be back as one of his children. She thought he would make a very good father. She had given him some of her jewellery so he would know it was her if she recognised it. Very Dalai Lama. She gave the rest to her granddaughter explaining, of course, she would be coming back to see her when she could.

Her granddaughter's response was as follows. 'It will be very nice see you, Lucia, but I'm not giving you back your things. They're mine now.'

She cheered up most of the other patients, sitting there like a little Buddha dispensing advice about this life and the next. There were several younger women there, who had young children, and found her a great comfort.

'You'll be alright,' she said, 'and if you're not, you can come back and be with them in some other form. Look at me, I'm ordering everything I want for my next life. A family that loves me and wants me to be with them. And money and cars. And a wonderful house in Italy, where I can sit in the sun and paint.'

Then there was hospital chaplain, a very down to earth Swedish woman, called Sieve. Lucia didn't cry much round me, but occasionally I'd find her closeted with Sieve in floods of tears. Sieve's beliefs had not until then encompassed reincarnation, but she found it all very interesting and they became firm friends. If nothing else Lucia believed in an afterlife, so they were on common ground there.

Towards the end Lucia was moved into a hospice. While she was being admitted I sat beside her reading the leaflet. It said the average stay was around twelve days. And twelve days is what she got. Her youngest son, Oliver, was coming over from Greece. Her daughter visited with the grandchildren. I read her a Harry Potter book which she hadn't managed to finish.

Together we looked up undertakers and planned the funeral. We settled on a firm that was run by women. Chose the songs. And, of course, we kept up an ongoing discussion on what she might meet on the other side.

'I'll let you know when I get there,' she assures me.

'Don't you dare go haunting me,' I say. 'You've given me enough trouble in this life.'

But, as you will see, she kept her word.

It was Lucia's last day and she was already more or less unconscious. It was only a matter of time. I had gone home to wash and make the final arrangements for the funeral, as her son would have to get back to the hotel as soon as possible.

I explain the situation to the undertaker.

'Are you sure you want to set the date?' They ask me. 'If your friend hasn't died yet?'

'She better bloody die, now I've got everything arranged,' I say.

I went back to the hospice to find Lucia's mother had arrived. I don't know quite how much she took in. Her other daughter was also in hospital suffering from cancer and she hadn't seen Lucia for months. But she sat there beside her and I made her hold Lucia's hand.

She went very quietly. Very quietly for her anyway. Dosed up on morphine. Slowly breathing her last.

We sat with her for a while. Her mother and me. Then the nurse came in and they sent us away while they tidied her up.

Washed and lying neatly in the bed she looked like a child asleep. Like the child her mother had abandoned to the spinster ladies all those years ago. Now her mother was here and the institutions in which she'd been carried to the end of her life were entirely benign. I felt as though a cycle had been properly completed, some kind of soul retrieval achieved.

The family retreated. Oliver had not yet arrived. So it was down to me to register her death. Lucia had changed her names several times so it was going to take a bit of working out. I found myself in an office with the registrar, a young woman. I explained the matter of the names and she asked me for details.

She said, 'You give me all the information. I'll show you what I've typed on the screen and then I'll print the death certificate.'

Linda Harper, Persephone Harper, Persephone Thompson, Persephone Harper, Lucia Carina. We did all that. She showed me the screen. I said everything was correct. She put a piece of paper in the printer and it began to print.

When she took the piece of paper out of the machine I knew something was wrong.

'What's the matter?' I ask.

'Look, I'm really sorry, I've never done this before,' she says.

The piece of paper is pink.

'I know what you've done,' I say. 'You've printed it on the birth certificate.'

'Yes, I'm really sorry,' she says.

'Don't worry. It wasn't you. I know who did that.'

She printed it again. This time on green paper.

I laughed all the way home. Lucia had let me know.

And that was not the only message she sent. Sieve was not with her when she died, but I sent her a message. She said she had gone into the loo and wasn't thinking about Lucia when the glass from her watch popped out and the watch stopped. About half an hour later she got my message and realised that was the moment when Lucia died.

Then there was the matter of the returning Taurean. Lucia hadn't told him about her illness because he was dealing with his own cancer scare and she didn't want to add to his emotional burden. But I was to tell him about the funeral. I sent a message and instructions about how to get to the crematorium.

On the day of the funeral I went into the undertakers to say a proper goodbye. I went with Will and Oliver. Oliver didn't want to see Lucia dead. He wanted to remember his mother as she was, so full of life and love and determination and always very aware of her appearance. But Will and I went in.

As I stood there I had this strange feeling that she was breathing, or at least giving the impression that her chest was rising and falling. I said what I needed in terms of saying goodbye and left. Will stayed. He wanted a bit of time with her on his own.

When he came out, I said, 'Did you think she looked as though she was breathing?'

162

'That was nothing,' he said. 'When you left she kept raising an eyebrow.'

We were neither of us surprised.

The undertaker had to go and do something in the office. The door to the outside locked automatically, so I asked if I could open it myself as her daughter was expected.

The bell rang. I went to the door. Instead of her daughter a man was standing outside with a map in his hand. I opened the door. He said my name. I said, 'Alan.' It was the Taurean, on his way to the crematorium.

He had been driving into Ipswich as per my instructions and wondered if he was coming the right way. He looked up and saw a funeral parlour. Thought, they'll know, I'll stop and ask. And he had arrived with us.

'I'm sure Lucia would like you to go in and say goodbye to her,' I say.

'I'd like that.'

Alan was with her for a while and came out looking quite emotional. 'We need a penny for the boatman. We need to make sure she gets to the other side.'

Everyone gets out their change but Alan has the brightest penny. 'Go, you give it to her,' I say. 'She'd like a man to pay the ferryman for her. She'd like it to be you.'

So off he goes and comes back grinning. 'I told her, don't give it to him 'til you get to the other side. He'll be Greek after all.'

Not very fair to the Greeks who had always been very generous with us, but at least he was getting into the spirit of things.

We went to the crematorium where a motley collection of her family, including the father of her children, my friends, two nurses from the hospital and Sieve. The children had chosen music that would send her dancing into the other world. I told them the story of the birth certificate. Sieve told the story of her broken watch. And we all sang *Will you go Lassie go...* to the general confusion of her mother and stepfather, who were probably expecting hymns.

The party was held in my garden where her grandchildren played under the apple tree and Sieve presented us with the most wonderful cake. Only her eldest son, Casper, was missing as someone had to keep the hotel running, but he was going to scatter her ashes on the sea in Greece so he would be finishing the ritual.

She died on a Wednesday, so by Thursday she was definitely invisible.

She left me her figure of the Cretan snake goddess which now sits on my mantelpiece together with a much more primitive goddess figure she had given me at Christmas when we were living in Crete.

But what does it all mean, I wonder now? We went on an incredible journey laced with Greek myth and magic. Like Theseus we travelled to the centre of the labyrinth and came out alive. We loved and lost and betrayed each other and plenty of other people. Somewhere along the line we lived up to the names we chose for ourselves or had chosen.

That was Lucia.

I hear her still. I see her sometimes. She still makes me laugh. The other voice is that of my sister.

---

*Remember me, Cassandra. Your sister. Remember. I was small and fat and angry and you wouldn't play with me. I was big and bright and beautiful and you wouldn't play with me. Now you're going to play with me. Play before the bloody lights go our forever. Play...*

*BROKEN*

---

**Orpheus**

*When Orpheus lost his wife Eurydice to a snakebite he went down into the underworld to beg Hades for her return. Hades granted him his wish on the understanding that he must walk back out into the light without turning to see if Eurydice was following him. He was nearly there but he could not hear her footsteps on the path behind him. So he turned. And watched. As she was drawn back into the dark.*

165

# VISIBLE

I have made two journeys back to Greece in the last few years. One was to Ithaca where the story of my name originates. I went with a friend who just wanted some time in the sun. I knew this was my opportunity. We stayed in Kefalonia, in Fiskardo, a little fishing village with Ithaca visible on the horizon.

We took two trips to Ithaca. The first was in a boat with about twenty other people. Then in a small motorboat hired by some friends who were staying in the apartment next door. That was the trip that mattered. We arrived in a small port and got out, not knowing how to get to the town which was the supposed site of Odysseus' palace. On the dock I found two Greek women and asked them the way – in Greek of course – and was generally directed up the hill. As we walked a pick-up truck stopped beside us. It was the same women and a male friend asking us if we'd like a lift. Thank the gods we took it. It would have taken us about an hour walking on the road.

Up in the town we were deposited by a café. It was a national holiday. Nothing much was open. But this turned out to be a café owned by the local mayor and we were treated like royalty, especially when I said my name was Penelope and I had come home. He gave us free beers and explained that it was *'Oxi nmera'* (No Day), the day on which the Greek Prime Minister told Mussolini he could not use Greek soil to park his troops and incurred the wrath of the Axis Powers. It was an auspicious day for all of us.

Later I went to the church and lit a candle for Lucia and for William, my Odysseus, and for my sister, my mother and father and anyone else who travelled in the land of the dead and had not yet returned to us.

166

We sailed back to the other island, feasted and danced into the night as it was my friend's birthday.

Three years later it was Crete. I went on a riding holiday with my two friends, Canny and Barbara. We stayed in a wonderful hotel in the mountains run by a Dutch woman and her Greek husband. Beautiful stables, lovely rooms with views out over the valley, fabulous food.

We rode up over the Dikteon Mountains, down onto the Lassithi Plateau, back up the mountains, down to the sea, round through the olive groves and back to the stables. It took us six days and we stayed in various other places but came back to the hotel every other day. The ride was spectacular and interesting but it is the people who made this journey for us.

On our first day we are met at a crossroads by a black-clad woman with whom I exchange the traditional greeting – much to my own satisfaction she seems to understand me. And as we leave she wishes us, '*Kalos dromos*' (Good road) and we feel our journey has been blessed. This happens again in a village on the next day.

And then there are the occasions when we need water for the horses. One woman starts emptying her entire water supply into a plastic bucket and all the family join in, along with most of the village children when they see the horses. The grandmother gives us three oranges to take with us. As we enter another village a woman runs down her garden with a hose before we have time to ask.

On one of the days our instructions say we will be alone in the mountains except for some 'rough but courteous shepherds'. We are very much on the lookout for those. We find one. He gives us water. He is from Pakistan.

I seemed to have mastered how to ask for water and for directions but was not always understood on other occasions. There was a day when we were leading our horses through a village and I decided we needed to know where we were in case we got lost and had to phone the stables about our general position.

There was a lovely old man sitting on a chair by a wall. I think I say in Greek, 'This village, what is it called?' He says, 'My name is Nico.' I say, 'My name is Penelope.' He tells me he is alone, his wife is dead. I say, 'I am alone also but what is the name of this place – *edo*?' He says, 'This is his house.'

I run after the others laughing and saying I think I might be on the way to a contract of marriage and we better get a move on. We never did find out the name of the village.

After our ride we go back to Agios Nikolaos and I meet people I haven't seen for thirty years. In my researches before we left I found evidence that both the villas Persey and I stayed in and the taverna were still extant. I emailed the villas and said, 'You may remember me?' and 'Did they have somewhere for us to stay for a couple of nights?'

The response was 'Yes,' but there was only one villa available and that happened to be the one I had lived in with the boys all those years ago. It felt a bit strange for a moment, but as ever I took it to be yet another indication that my journey had meaning – even if it was entirely fabricated by myself.

We hire a car from the airport and drive to Agios Nikolaos. I drive on the right-hand side in a left-hand drive car. The results are much the same as they were in Corfu more than thirty years before, with my two passengers screaming at me to get away from the edge and avoid parked cars. Thank god they did.

After some confusion driving through a half remembered town we arrive at the villa. As we walk up to my house there is a man working in the garden. He looks very like my old landlord and I wonder what elixir the

Greeks have discovered to keep them young? It is, of course, his son. Later the whole family turns up and, although they look a little older, it is much the same as it always was and a delight to see them.

We go to the taverna. As I walk up the steps and say my name the owner, Stathis, says, 'It's been a very long time!!' Now whether he remembers me or whether the grapevine has been at work, it is difficult to say. But the greeting is genuine. I ask him if Manolis is around? Oh yes, he was here earlier, he will come tonight. We have some lunch and beer. Meet his charming son and daughter. And go for a swim on a fairly deserted beach in water you can see through.

The evening comes and we are back in the taverna. Earlier I had seen Stathis making the phone call – 'Get over here, big brother, one of your women has arrived.'

Now whether he could remember me or not, Manolis makes the perfect entrance. Walking towards me across the taverna saying, 'My beautiful woman.'

I wouldn't have recognised him in the street but he is immediately familiar. And still a very handsome man. I ask him if he still plays the bouzouki? He tells us he will be in the bar.

Later he plays to us and plies us with raki. 'Are you married?' he asks me.

'No, Manolis, I never married.'

'Then I will marry you,' he says.

I remind him that he has a wife. He always had a wife. But it's always nice to be asked. He is wonderful and outrageous and clearly hopes I will make love with him.

'I like to make love,' he says.

I know. He shows us pictures of himself with various women. All of him when he was young. I don't find myself in the gallery but he wants a copy of the pictures I've brought with me. He makes it very clear that he would make love with any or all of us if that's what we want. And we all laugh and celebrate his enthusiasm and drive back into the night giggling.

I wake in the night and find myself wandering the house. I think of myself all those years ago. Still in shock from William's death. Still processing Charlotte leaving as she did. Still dealing with my mother's stroke. I was a mess and Manolis was kind. He let me inhabit his bar for a year and let my children fall asleep there. And he touched me. I think that's what I needed most. His hands wandering over me, reminding me I was still alive. Him calling to me with his music. I look in the mirror and think, *Manolis saved my life.*

On the way out of Iraklion in the car we failed to find the road to Knossos but, of course, I have a monument I think my friends will like much better. On the first morning in Agios I take them up into the mountains to the ruined city of Lato, where I had once taken the boys.

We wander around identifying banqueting halls, the water features, a theatre, a temple and small solid houses with shelves and places for storing the jars. As the morning goes on a few other tourists arrive and a party of schoolchildren, but it is never crowded and there are no official guides.

Now we are wandering the tracks behind the villas and the village looking for the *SITE OF APHRODITE.* I know vaguely where it is but not how to get there. Our landlady has said she thinks the road is lost. First I ask a man with a child, but he says he's not from round here. Then, just as we are about to give up, I meet a woman walking the road. I greet her. Explain – at least I think I explain – that I lived here thirty-years ago and ask her the way to the site. She says something to the effect that it is difficult and then

170

suddenly she beckons me and walks off through the ruined houses at the edge of the village and in amongst the olive trees. We follow. She walks us across stony ground. Past a fiercely barking dog. I fall onto a steel post and cut my leg. And then she points and we can see it. The rows of finished stone. A grove of trees that aren't all olive trees. She comes no further, leaving us to our visit. Just points the best way back to the village. And she is gone.

All of us find this place enchanting. There is a kind of peace there that we haven't found anywhere else. Even Barbara, who prefers to see most religious monuments from outside, says she feels it. Canny and I go and put offerings on what may have been the altar.

I put a sprig of rosemary that Manolis gave me. A stone. A little bit of blood from the cut on my leg. And say thank you. I don't think I have got the love I thought I wanted when I spoke to Aphrodite thirty years ago. Not the one true love. But I have learnt to accept love in all its forms and now I am here again. Seems to me that I've had all the love I needed and learnt not to make value judgements.

Canny remarks on how feminine the energy feels. Quiet. Enclosing. Secretive. Barbara notes that there are other offerings. People from the village are still using it as a shrine.

On the way back through the village we see the woman again and I thank her. I tell her how beautiful the place is. She smiles. Such a warm, open smile. And we feel that we have been led to the sanctuary by its guardian. A rare privilege.

I feel I want to thank Manolis too. He was a good friend to me all those years ago. I give him a card and a tatty guitar keyring and get another Greek to write *FOR A GOOD FRIEND*. I hope he gets the message. Later I send him photographs. The ones of us both sitting in the bar thirty years ago. Him and Canny and Barbara sitting in the same place, he is probably sitting on the same chair. Also some very fine portraits of himself now. I tell him what a handsome man he still is. I thank him again for his kindness. He is not a stupid man. He will understand.

But what is most extraordinary is how I feel when I get home. Something has happened. It may be seeing Manolis again. Did he still have something that was mine? Was he one of my keepers? It may be seeing the two families and how well they have survived and being welcomed back. It may be rediscovering the temple to Aphrodite. It may be yet another journey with two wonderful friends, who see things for what they are and make me laugh.

Whatever it is I walk the streets at home smiling to myself. I inhabit my body. I look at my friends in the pub and refuse to be annoyed when they behave badly. I feel as though I have at last – as Persey/Lucia suggested at the start – come back to myself. Become myself. Now that was a journey worth making.

*In the car*
*On the way home*
*From the funeral*

*He*
*Who saw you*
*Lifted from the wet earth*
*Your dark hair*
*Blood stuck*

*Our brother said*

*It must be worse*
*In time of war*
*To see so many*
*So many of your friends*
*Dead*

*And I*

*Who heard you last alive*
*On the telephone*

*Your sister*

*I saw then*
*An orchard*
*The grass left long*
*To catch the falling fruit*
*Bodies under the trees*

*Your body there*
*Under the apple tree*
*In the orchard of our childhood*

*ELMSTED 1977*

173

## LIKE TO READ MORE WORK LIKE THIS?

Then sign up to our mailing list and download our free collection of short stories, *Magnetism*. Sign up now to receive this free e-book and also to find out about all of our new publications and offers.

Sign up here:
   http://eepurl.com/gbpdVz

# PLEASE LEAVE A REVIEW

Reviews are so important to writers. Please take the time to review this book. A couple of lines is fine.

Reviews help the book to become more visible to buyers. Retailers will promote books with multiple reviews. This in turn helps us to sell more books... And then we can afford to publish more books like this one.

Leaving a review is very easy.

Go to https://bit.ly/3QCemnJ, scroll down the left-hand side of the Amazon page and click on the "Write a customer review" button.

# OTHER WRITING BY PEPPY BARLOW

Peppy Barlow is a founder member of the Woven Theatre Company, set up to encourage women's writing in East Anglia: www.woventheatre.co.uk.

Her plays include:

A family trilogy – *Missing*, *Mothering Sunday* and *Broken* – variously produced by The Wolsey Theatre, Eye Theatre and Woven

*Dead End* – The Wolsey Theatre and the Union Theatre Southwalk, adapted and toured as Grasping at Shadows by Woven.

*The Sutton Hoo Mob* – Eastern Angles 1992 and 2004

*Shadows in the Doorway* – BBC Radio 4 1992

*Turning the Tide* – Open Space Theatre 2010

*Philip Thicknesse; Friend or Foe* – written with Sally Wilden, a site-specific production at Landguard Fort Felixstowe produced by Woven in 2017

*Gainsborough and the Modern Woman* – written with Sally Wilden and toured by Woven 2022

She has also written several short films: *Driftwood*, *Like a Bullet*, *Half Empty*, *Nobody Asked*, *Family Tree* and *Self Assessment* – all but *Driftwood* produced and directed by Howard Smith.

# OTHER PUBLICATIONS BY BRIDGE HOUSE

## The House on Schellberg Street

### *by Gill James*

Renate Edler loves to visit her grandmother in the house on
Schellberg Street. She often meets up with her friend Hani
Gödde who lives nearby. This year, though, it is not to be.
Just a few weeks after a night when synagogues are burned
and businesses owned by Jews are looted, Renate finds out
a terrible secret about her family.

At a time when the world is at war and the horrors of the
Holocaust are slowly becoming apparent, Renate has to leave
behind her home and her friends, and become somebody she
never thought she could be.

The house on Schellberg Street needs to stay strong. Will it and
those who work in it be strong enough? Will Renate ever feel
at home again? And what of those left behind?

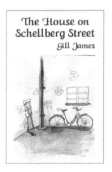

"A must-read for anyone studying World war II. Anyone who
enjoyed *The Boy with the Striped Pyjamas* will love it." *(Amazon)*

Order from Amazon:
ISBN: 978-1-910542-23-1 (paperback)
978-1-910542-24-8 (ebook)

**Chapeltown Books**

## Clara's Story: a Holocaust Biography

### *by Gill James*

Clara will not be daunted. Her life will not end when her beloved husband dies too young. She will become a second mother to the young children who live away from home at a rather special school – a particular class of disabled children growing up in Nazi Germany.

*Clara's Story: a Holocaust Biography* is the second story in the Schellberg Cycle. It might be described as a tragedy or it might be described as a story of survival. In the end it is up to the reader or even Clara herself to decide.

"The social history starting before World War 1, and continuing to the present day, was extremely interesting and Clara herself had the attitude that where there's hope there's life. A well-written and thought-provoking book." *(Amazon)*

Order from Amazon:
ISBN: 978-1-910542-33-0 (paperback)
978-1-910542-34-7 (ebook)

**Chapeltown Books**

# Girl in a Smart Uniform

## *by Gill James*

*Girl in a Smart Uniform* is the third book in the
Schellberg Cycle, a collection of novels inspired by a
bundle of photocopied letters that arrived at a small
cottage in Wales in 1979. The letters give us first-hand
insights into what life was like growing up in Germany
in the 1930s and 1940s.

It is the most fictional of the stories to date, though
some characters, familiar to those who have read the
first two books, appear again here. Clara Lehrs, Karl
Schubert and Dr Kühn really existed. We have a few, a
very few, verifiable facts about them. The rest we have
had to find out by repeating some of their experiences
and by using the careful writer's imagination.

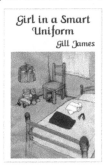

"The book is well written and easy to read. The girl's home life
is complicated and there are some moving develop-ments
involving her brothers. Thoroughly worth reading!" *(Amazon)*

Order from Amazon:
ISBN: 978-1-910542-10-1 (paperback)
978-1-910542-11-8 (ebook)

**Chapeltown Books**

Lightning Source UK Ltd.
Milton Keynes UK
UKHW021351271122
412909UK00012B/228